FULL TIMING IN A MO
by Gary Burfield-W

Copyright 2017 Gary Burfield-Wallis

Contents

Background	5
Careless words.	8
Fate is in control.	13
Wild camping.	18
First time out.	22
New year new life.	26
Freedom.	29
Floods.	32
Dorset.	37
Hurricanes.	41
Deserted.	43
A long stopover.	47
Tea in Cardiff.	51
Huskies.	56
Rally.	58
The onesie dance.	62
Problems Sorted.	65
Flat Tyre.	67
Whoops That's blocked it.	72
STOP!	75
More disasters.	78
North.	83

Scotland.	88
Half way.	92
Time To Head South.	96
Nudists.	99
South of South.	102
Change of plan.	107
Broken Bed.	112
Mountain Pass.	114
Opposites.	118
Christmas.	125
Sightseeing.	133
New Year.	137
Not Again.	142
Delivery Day.	147
Newark Motorhome show.	151
National Motorhome Show.	155
Enhancements & Planning.	158
Bang.	161
Fun	167
Shropshire the forgotten county	174
Water Management	181
Southwards	185
The channel crossing	188
Germany	190

France	193
Spain	200
Insurance	205
Old Friends	207
Rural Spain	210
Christmas	214
About the author	215

Background

At 50 years of age, it was time to completely turn my life upside down and head in a truly terrifying and yet exciting direction. I just didn't know it yet.

I had been married to Ann for nearly 10 years in a small three bedroom terraced house in West Sussex where I had lived for four or five years previous to our wedding. I was never one to move very often and absolutely detested the idea of having to uproot and have my established routines messed around with. So what was about to come would be a massive surprise and shock to me.

When I think back, I realise that the sequence of events actually begin in the spring of 2013. Business had finally been bearing some decent fruit and we decided we should go on that long awaited cruise we had always wanted to do but could not afford. So I booked us a Mediterranean cruise.

We flew out to Barcelona in Spain where we boarded this enormous five star floating hotel. We really couldn't get over just how big this thing was. Our bags were taken from us and we were able to do a bit of exploring around this fantastic ship (although to annoy anyone listening I kept calling it a boat) while they delivered our bags to the room and made it ready for us. Once done, we went up to our balcony room and met our steward who was to look after us during our stay.

He was a tall African American young gentleman who insisted on calling us Mr Gary and Miss Ann. This felt somewhat wrong as it had undertones of the American deep south plantations of the seventeenth century. Andrew was a brilliant steward and nothing was too much trouble. In a way he was a little scary as no matter what you asked him for it would mysteriously appear in our room very soon after asking but not once did we see him put it there.

Our cruise was to take us to seven ports in four countries over the next 12 days which really didn't give us much time at each port with the exception of Venice where we had an overnight stop as well.

To maximise the time we had I pre-booked tours at most of the ports, guessing that this was probably the best way to sample each place and be guaranteed that we didn't get back late for the departure by doing our own thing.

It's on these tours that, I suppose, I started to rekindle my desire to travel and explore that I had as a teenager and young man. The tours were all too brief really, time ashore was limited, but did give you a brief taste of the life, culture and history of the country. It also prompted great discussions between us over where we would like to return to for a much longer visit.

My intentions for this book is to tell our story about how, we as an average couple, living an average lifestyle, broke through our comfort barrier to discover a whole new wonderful life. But I also want it to be so much more. I am also hoping you will find it packed full of advice and help with motor-homing and provide some great travel tips and places worth visiting and those to avoid. But most of all I hope it will inspire some of you to do the same, it's so worth it.

Careless words.

My new found desire really started to give me itchy feet and later that same year was another opportunity to travel. I treated Ann to a long weekend trip to southern Ireland as a birthday present. A place neither of us had been before. This time though we would drive so we could take as much time as we wanted to explore.

In the early stages of our journey, the first half hour actually, Ann says "Wouldn't it be a good idea to buy a camper-van then we won't have to kennel the dogs but they can come with us?" Our two Huskies, Ellie and Sasha, really didn't cope well in kennels and we hated having to leave them.

Those that know me, will know that whilst I may not appear to be giving any thought to such a query (or any thought to anything really) will know that somewhere in a dark and probably scary corner of my mind this will be being analysed and processed, quite often, unbeknown to my conscious mind.

By the time we reached our hotel (Athenaeum House Hotel) in Waterford this passing thought had developed and grown to the size that my brain had decided can no longer be processed in the background and had pushed it into my conscious thought processes and I was giving it, on and off, some serious consideration.

We loved our few days in Ireland and visited some fascinating places and museums. While visiting a lovely old market town we were told about a very beautiful waterfall and magic road we should go and see. This involved a drive up into the local mountains which were absolutely stunning despite the low cloud.

This didn't help to put the camper-van idea aside as we both agreed the dogs would love it up here. I also had forgotten how much I loved the mountains and having spent many hours, many years back, walking and camping in the mountains of England and Wales the yearning to be able to go up into the mountains again returned with some earnest and owning a camper-van would make that very possible.

The magic road was a bit of a let down really as we couldn't find the right place to let the car roll uphill despite it being signposted. Never mind, it was fun trying.

On the journey home, some 12 hours of traveling, we began to discuss the idea further and quite favourably I might add. I had rationalised that we really could not afford to run two vehicles but if we got one of a size I could get into a car park, we could use it as our only vehicle. After all the amount of local trips I take are pretty much non existent now that one of my sons had left for University and the other lived with his mother and so Dad's free taxi service was not used much at all anymore.

Over the next few days back at home, I started to do some research into this camper-van idea and the idea started to grow into something much much bigger as I started to read about "full timers", those that have moved out of their house to live permanently in a motorhome.

This idea was very nice and a lovely, but the cost of a motorhome was going to be a major stumbling block and as a result I kind of put the idea to one side for one day in the future.

Within a few days of this set aside, I had an appointment with my bank to discuss how they can save me money on my account. This was a very short meeting as I pointed out, within about 30 seconds, that their new account will actually cost me more.

As I was about to leave the young lady I was talking to mentioned, in a very casual way, was I aware that I have a £25,000 facility on the account if I needed it. Bang! I was stopped dead in my tracks but not only that the, previously set aside, motorhome idea came smashing its way through my thoughts screaming very loudly that it's still there and here is a solution. The thought was so loud that it kind of caught me off guard. Sometimes I hate the way my subconscious works.

I told the young lady that no, I was not aware and what would be the repayments on that? She typed some stuff into her computer and then removed a sheet of paper from the printer and handed it to me. Nearly £600 per month over 5 years. I thanked her and left.

Now there is no way I could afford a repayment of that size in my current situation BUT, if we were to become full timers without the cost of the rent, council tax, water rates, gas, electricity, phone, sky plus and probably a few other things, we are going to have so much spare money it would be ridiculous. Yes there will be other costs for example site fees, diesel, gas etc but there is no way they are going to be as large as the current ones put together. Even if it all worked out the same it wouldn't have mattered now as my dream of traveling and seeing the world that I have had since my late teens was now a very real possibility.

Over the next few weeks, I start to look much, much deeper into this idea with lots of research. It begins to dawn on me that, so far, I have not found any negatives to embarking on this crazy adventure. We have also begun to discuss this plan, oh yeah it's a plan now not just an idea, with friends and family.

This is where I expected to get comments and advice on why this is a stupid idea and we would be mad to do it. Oh how wrong was I. Not a single person we spoke to thought this and everyone said it was a great idea and we should go for it.

It seems a bit strange to admit, but the lack of reasons not to do it started alarm bells ringing in my head. Surely there must be a downside to this. I became a little obsessed with finding at least one or two reasons. Then it dawned on me, Ann had not actually seen inside of one of these things (neither had I really) and when she does she is not going to be quite so keen, as its going to be a lot smaller to live in than were both used to.

A couple of weeks later we happened to be in North Wales taking a weekend break with a couple of friends. Yet more traveling, I had traveled more and seen more places in the last few months than I had in total over the last several years and was loving it. It's here in Wales I found a motor home dealer just around the corner to where we are staying so suggested we take a look. All four of us drove round there and started to wander around peering in the windows of all these motor homes. We eventually found one that was open so in we went for a look. I'm thinking wait for it, its about to all come crashing down.

WRONG AGAIN! Ann absolutely loved it and sees nothing but good things and marvels at the storage space and how clever they have been and she can still do her baking as it has an oven.

Oh for crying out loud, this is not meant to go like this. Just goes to prove that the female mind is impossible to predict.

Fate is in control.

This chapter was supposed to be titled "THE TRIAL". The idea was to hire a Motorhome for a couple of weeks to see how it all worked and if there were any major issues. However it seems that fate, the cosmos, a higher entity, sprits or some other unseen force had other plans for me and wasn't going to let me mess around with doing trial runs or any other manner of things to delay the inevitable whether I liked it or not.

A week or so later we were chatting to one of our friends about our plans and the bank rings me up out of the blue asking if I would like the £25,000 loan at a greatly reduced interest rate, in fact quite a stupidly low interest rate. After a short amount of spluttering, umming and arring I reasoned why not give it a try? Chances are, when it comes down to the actual checks, they no doubt have to do, there will be some sort of issue. So agree to pop in that afternoon to sign the papers.

I arrived at the bank I had a brief chat, signed the papers and in about 10 minutes had £25,000 in my bank account. No further checks, no nothing, they just gave me the money. Whoops that wasn't supposed to happen either.

So now my plans changed a little and thought we could start seriously looking in January as soon as we have done the 'trial run', maybe even look during the trial as we travel up the country.

The following week I had to make a rare visit to a client down in Southampton and since I knew of a large Motorhome dealer down there (from the extensive research I had been doing) I thought I would take the opportunity of being in the area to pop in for a peruse of some motorhomes and try and get a bit of advice.

Arriving at the dealers, I went straight to the showroom office and chatted to a very helpful chap called Graham who listened carefully to what my plans were and made notes of the list of 'must haves' on my motorhome. I really had done a lot of research. Almost all on my list were no problem at all with the exception of the French style bed and 6 belted seats, however he said, let's go and have a look around. Ah ha up yours fate I've found a problem.

<u>Shopping list</u>

French style bed

6 seat belts

Solar panel

2 leisure batteries

Winterised tanks

2 gas bottles

We looked at four or five different motorhomes but for one reason or another none were suitable but I was at least getting a very good idea of what was possible and what's not. He finally showed me one that was almost just right, except the French style bed. But it did have two lounges, a rear U shaped lounge, which would convert into a double bed, as well as a lounge in the centre which housed the four rear traveling seats facing each other with a choice of two tables between them. Oh come on, two tables to choose from, now that's just showing off.

I pointed out that having to make up the bed each night was a big issue and would drive me nuts in no time. But, he pointed out, that if there is only the two of you most of the time you can leave the bed in the rear made up all the time. Ah! Good point. And if we have guests staying it gives us the extra lounge space, if needed, by turning it back into a lounge.

Now Ann really needs to see this so I give her a call using Apple's Face Time (my turn to show off) as I wanted her to have a quick look at it and decide if she wants to come down and see it.

Having made me show her just about every nook and cranny and asked Graham several questions which he answered to her satisfaction she announces she doesn't need to come all the way down there to see it as she has seen it now and is quite happy it will be just fine and its up to me.

Oh for crying out loud, not again, it wasn't supposed to go like that (I really must stop trying to second guess how things are supposed to go, I'm no good at it). So I clarify with Graham that all the extras I need can be fitted by them and how much extra it will be. His answer meant the price of the motorhome plus the extras means I won't need any further financing. I will have everything I need. Ann is happy with it. It has low milage. Graham, unhelpfully, points out that because it's a 6 berth with 6 traveling belts it will be easy to sell and won't loose much value, if any, if it doesn't work out for us.

Damn, I can't find a reason not to proceed and believe me I had several minutes having a big row in my head over this, which I consequently lost and found myself pulling out of the dealership wondering "what the hell just happened" having just paid a deposit.

So that was it. I had been manipulated by whatever unseen force that had now clearly taken over my life. Ripping up, in front of my face, my plans for trials and lots more research and proceeding months earlier than I intended. We would take delivery of our new home in 2 weeks time.

The next 2 weeks turned out completely manic as we start to try to sell nearly everything we have and make trip after trip down the local amenity tip to throw everything else away. After about the third or fourth trip down to the tip they all knew my name and what I was doing and came to help unload the car and put the stuff in the correct sections.

Selling our furniture was not that simple as we didn't want anyone actually taking anything until after Christmas as we had already made plans for family to come to us for the festive period. So lots of promises were made and dates arranged for the period between Christmas and New Year with Ann keeping a very organised record of who is having what and when.

Over Christmas we had lots of visitors and I felt sorry for the poor souls who weren't allowed to leave either without a promise to return with a van and buy stuff from us or at the very least take various nicks and knacks with them there and then.

In no time at all the house no longer felt like home as all our stuff not sellable had been thrown away.

Wild camping.

Two weeks pass very quickly and my step daughter Amanda takes me down to the dealers to collect our new motor home. Before being allowed to drive it away, I was given a full induction which covered off all I needed to know on how everything worked. It really was an awful lot to take in and wished Ann had come with me as she will have remembered different things to me. After this, while sorting out the paperwork and, oh yeah, paying for it, they prepared it for driving away which included giving me a full tank of fuel, which was a nice surprise.

It's strange that whilst I have driven so many different vehicles of all sizes this one seemed so much bigger and for the first time since passing my test I was actually a bit nervous as I pulled off the forecourt on to the busy main A road.

I had programmed my Sat Nav to not take me the easy long way home via the motorways, but the shortest route going directly across country. My reasoning was to get used to this beast of a vehicle whilst on my own and not being told what I am doing wrong. As I settled into driving I realised that it's not all that big and very easy to handle and I soon became very comfortable with it. If the worry of driving something much bigger than a car is stopping you from getting a motorhome then don't let it. Trust me, you very quickly realise, the bigger the vehicle the easier it is to drive.

The next few days proved to be a very enlightening experience. Because the insurance I had arranged for it was a special "Full Timers" insurance I had to live in it starting that day, even if it was parked outside the house we had been renting for the last 10+ years. The first night was excellent, the best I had slept in years, and I even overslept which is something I just don't EVER do. So there was a big plus to start with.

Thank heavens I did this when it was getting dark quite early in the day as I discovered I had no idea how to turn the lights on in the living area and had to ring the dealer to ask. Fortunately they were still open and very kindly explained where to look. Oh yeah, now that's obvious, now feeling very stupid I said thank you and hung up.

The first morning I found out the importance of having spare fuses as I plugged in a phone charger with a dodgy wire (it turned out) and it blew a fuse and I had no power to the 12 volt sockets and worse still the control panel didn't display how much life I had in the batteries. This was the start of so much to learn. Fortunately a neighbour helped me out here with a spare fuse and even later in the day turned up with a pack of them he had bought for me. Thanks Rob.

A few days later I worked out if I use the tank heaters that were installed to stop them from freezing overnight then they will completely drain both my leisure batteries which led on to discovering that even if its a grey, drizzly, winters day the solar panel still does it's thing and soon at least had internal lights. The following night, I worked out that even if it is zero degrees the insulation around the tanks will mean they still don't freeze.

I think it's just a question of keeping an eye on the forecast and if the temperature is expected to drop well below zero then ensure we are on a site with electric hook up. Problem solved.

There is something oddly fun about waking in the morning to a freezing cold room, hopping out of bed and whacking the heating on and then diving back under the nice warm covers and wait for it all to warm up. Unless the urgency in my bladder insists sooner. Thank heavens it doesn't take too long to at least take the chill off.

I spend the next several weeks, as well as over Christmas, in my van pretty much refusing to enter the house with the exception of meal times. I really didn't want to be there any more as my nice organised life in the house had been totally upset and it no longer felt comfortable. I quickly got very comfortable in the van though, and found working in it to be no problem at all. The gas heater worked very well and I was nice and warm although having the heating on all day, it was winter after all, meant I was getting through a bottle of gas every 3 days. Luckily, there was a Calor centre just 3 minutes drive down the road so had to take a drive down there to get a replacement.

We slowly started to introduce our 2 Huskies to it with them taking it in turns to spend the night with me. They seemed to settle in to this surprisingly quickly and was very enthusiastic to get in when it was their turn.

I took the opportunity whilst still having a postal address to order a few more things off the internet.

Outside silver screen which turned out to be a most excellent buy as they helped to keep the heat in very, very well and, as I was to find out later in the year, keep the heat out. They also served to completely stop the condensation problem. Don't try to scrimp on this one it will be one of your most important assets and quality is the most important aspect. Some people use internal screens and indeed the do keep the cold and heat out but do nothing to stop the condensation.

WiFi booster which I used to connect to the WiFi in the house and has since turned out very useful when on sites where their WiFi didn't quite reach the pitch we were on or only had WiFi available at reception. I found https://www.motorhomewifi.com has the best solution for this.

Boxes, lots of boxes, the ones with lids and various sizes to help organise stuff in the cupboards and under seat storage. I was doing very well and pleased with myself getting my bits and pieces all organised and finding a place for everything until Ann decided to rearrange it all as she needed particular places for unnecessary items like food.

First time out.

Whilst I was pretty busy on a day to day basis with work I was still just outside the house, still in the same place I have been for the last 10 years but itching to get out on the road and start really using our motorhome. It occurred to me that I had no idea what is going to happen when we got to a site (wild camping would be no different to what I was doing now so that didn't bother me).

That was it, still the wrong side of Christmas, a long time before we actually leave for good, well only a few weeks but it felt like a long time, the decision was made, we were going to get away for a few days to a site not too far away but far enough to make it worth it. A bit like a mini adventure.

So I booked us a few nights away at Chertsey Camping and Caravanning Club Site. Ann loads up our motorhome just enough stuff on board for us to do this, wanting to still keep stuff in the house as we needed to get through Christmas yet. I thought this was a tiny bit annoying as was not really a full test of what we were going to embark on in the new year. But hey she was the boss.

Thanks to the marvel of the sat-nav we found the place no trouble at all and are given a very warm welcome and taken round to our pitch. We are given a couple of choices and I chose the one that I think will have a good view when it gets light in the morning based on the what sounded like a river close by. The EHU (Electric Hook Up) was easy enough to do and the pitch was nice and level so that was that concern dealt with.

It's a lovely riverside camp site nestled within the suburbs on the banks of the River Thames with easy access to central London by public transport, an ideal place to use as a base for those London sightseeing trips.

I was very disappointed with the site wifi. Whilst I could get a connection no problem, it was so painfully slow that I thought an old 56k dial up modem would have been faster. Never mind all of the four mobile sims I had, had good 3G or 4G signal so carrying on with work was no issue. I know four sounds a bit overboard but I needed to ensure that wherever we were I could get connected to the internet as I needed to work uninterrupted at all times.

Over the next two days we did a little exploring and the girls enjoyed the walks along the banks of the Thames, as did we. One evening we went to the Kingfisher public house just over the bridge and enjoyed a lovely meal leaving the girls alone for the first time in the van. We had closed all the blinds and turned the power off as we left in the hope that if it's dark and they can't see anything to destroy, they won't. When we got back we were both very pleased with them and by the look of the two sets of bleary eyes looking at us I would say they just slept the whole time. Brilliant I think this full timing thing might just work out okay.

We met a lovely couple who were there with their caravan who gave me a great bit of advice about emptying our toilet cassette. "When you remove the cap to empty it don't put the cap down on the side of the drain point. A fair few new people make this mistake and then knock it off down the hole where it gets stuck. Not only can you not retrieve it but it blocks it up as well."

After a couple of days we were reluctantly due to go back home. I had downloaded and was looking at a Motor Home Parking App called All Motorhome Parkings – Campercontact and had spotted a wild camping spot between us and home just off the M25/A3 junction at Ockham. We just couldn't resist and had to go and give and it a try, proper wild camping, not just outside my house like when you're a kid and your mum lets you camp in the garden but real camping.

It turned out to be a very interesting experience. The site is a forestry commission car park that has a cafe on it and seemed to be very popular with the local tradesmen and drivers. Most of the site is not level at all but we did find a spot that was near enough.

Having walked the girls through the forest, discovered the TV reception was not very good, no wifi I could get onto, even with my booster, but I did have a good enough 3G signal. it was time to get the bed ready and settle down.

After a short while we started to realise it's also a very popular place after dark with "Doggers" (If you don't know what that is then trust me you don't really want to know) and has lots of people hanging around in cars and flashing their lights at each other. Ann was quite worried about this but I just found it all amusing. I even suggested we open the blinds and put on a bit of a show, to show them all how it should be done but Ann was having none of that "you dirty old man" she told me.

Ellie the oldest of the girls really proved to us at one point that we will be very safe wherever we go. Someone must have walked past the van a bit too close for her liking as she shot up and started growling in a way we have never seen before, she really meant business. This made me quite happy no one is going to trouble us and promptly fell asleep. Ann on the other hand didn't sleep well and told me the following morning that the activities outside went on till nearly day break.

Having had a very nice breakfast and a cappuccino at the cafe I got chatting to the lad that works there who was busy picking up litter and other unsavoury used items. Turns out he is not paid to do this but does it in his break, as he doesn't want the place looking a mess and putting off visitors. It was really nice to find someone and particularly a young someone who is making an effort off his own back. He also told me they would like a lot more motorhomes to visit as if they have enough regularly visiting it might just put a damper on the night time activities they suffer from.

To be fair none of the other users of this car park bothered us at all and as far as I could tell kept well away from us even though we were just about smack bang in the middle.

New year new life.

I decided I did not want to see the new year in at the house and our old life, but wanted to see it in as part of our new life that was due to start properly just a mere 6 days into the new year.

Having already experienced a Camping & Caravanning Club site I thought we should try a Caravan Club site this time, since I had paid membership for both of them, might as well make use of both of them. Having looked on their website I decided to book us in to the Littlehampton site for a few days spanning the new year.

It was a nice site, well kept and clean and the wardens were lovely and friendly with lots of advice. Apparently it's just a 30 minute walk into the town centre which is right on the seafront with promenade, beach and pier but seeing as the weather was not very nice and we were only there for a couple of days we didn't bother to go exploring.

Having told them all about starting full timing in the new year I was warned to keep that to ourselves as apparently it is against their rules and the club is for holidays only. It was to be the one and only time we used the club and when it was time to renew I let it lapse. They did call me to try to get me to renew and it appears the ones who try to sell you membership are unaware of their own rules and regulations.

After lunch and a pint at the Locomotive Pub just over the other side of the level crossing we had our usual quiet seeing in the new year together and were quite content with this sitting comfortably in our new home watching the TV.

Not long after sunrise of the new year Sasha, the youngest of our two huskies, stands by the door making those lovely noises dogs make when they are about to be sick. Quick as a flash I sling the door open, without putting her lead on, breaking another rule, and she jumps straight out. Immediately she stops her retching sounds, looks up at me and then legs it.

By the time I have got something on my feet and a coat, it was poring with rain, she has disappeared completely. The next few hours are spent searching the site and a large area of fields and streets in the area but not a sign of her anywhere.

Eventually, just before lunch, my phone rings and the lady on the phone says they have found Sasha. Having worked out where they are I set off to go get her. She was quite a distance away and had crossed over a very swollen and fast moving river, how she didn't end up in that I'll never know as she tends not to be that bright and over curious.

After calling the lady back for further instructions I eventually find them with her husband hanging on to a very wet and muddy dog. This is when I get the whole story. Apparently on their way to wherever it was these kind people had gone, Sasha had run out in the road in front of them and was hit by their car being unable to stop because of the wet roads. They never got a chance to see if she was alright as she got up and just ran off. It's on their return back they spotted her again and coaxed her over to them.

Having thanked and given them a small reward I walked her back to the site trying to work out if she had any injuries. I couldn't quite work out if she was limping on and off or not. Back in the van she was dried off and we had a good look at her and could only see what looked like a small cut above her eye which could of been sustained in any number of ways not necessary from being hit by a car.

Having fed her she then slept all afternoon and through the night. Next morning she was completely back to normal with no signs of her previous days adventures. I on the other hand ached like hell. Flipping dog.

Oh well adventure over back to the old house for the last few days.

Freedom.

The big day finally arrived and we waved bye bye to the old house. Well I didn't, I just drove off without even giving it a final glance. At last we were now officially full timers with no address, no bills, and no worries (well not as many as we had).

Well I say no address. The truth is you can not have an address and own a vehicle. So we used Ann's dads address for the vehicle registration and driving license. The insurance company was a little more helpful and used the address as a care of address understanding that we don't actually live there but in our motorhome.

It was odd. I didn't feel worried that we had just burned all our bridges and headed off into a very unsure future, which you would have thought I should have felt. No instead I felt as though a load of worries had just been lifted off my shoulders and the road ahead had promise and all manner of possibilities. I was genuinely excited by it.

The original plan was to take my oldest son, Nathaniel, back to university at Bournemouth first then on to a site nearby for our first stop. That was the plan and would have happened except for two major changes. 1. Nat was picked up by a friend before the new year so he could get back and drink vast quantities of alcohol with his mates at uni to celebrate the new year and 2. The site we were booked in rang to cancel our booking because they were flooded out.

No problem. I looked up where else we can stay near Bournemouth and found Black Lion Camping & Caravan Park. Which is a Camping & Caravanning Club certified site. You have to be a member to stop there. If you're not a member, no problem, you can join there.

We found the place no problem and were greeted by a very friendly owner who took me to look at the pitches. There were five to choose from (that was all of them, seems we will be the only ones there) all with brand new electric hook ups which I am then told is charged per unit (This worked out very expensive in the end but I had no idea at the time). I decide that we will take the first pitch which was close to a water tap. He also points out where the CDP (Chemical Disposal Point, where you empty your toilet cassette) and the toilets and showers, and finaly the best place to walk the dogs. There was no chance of flooding there as the field had very good drainage and higher up than the surrounding fields etc.

All looked good so we paid our fees and got set up for the next two weeks. The dog walk was really quite good and went around the site and through a well marked out wooded area. Having walked the dogs, I thought I would check out the showers. Oh dear, not only were they not heated, not good in January, but they had obviously not been cleaned in quite a while. Reporting back Ann decided she would go down and clean them herself so she could have a shower. To say she was not happy when she got back was an understatement. It appeared the hot water only lasted a few minutes then turned stone cold. Just strip washes in the van for us for now on then. We do have a shower in the van but with only a 45 litre tank it doesn't go very far so it's just easier to have a strip wash.

Saturday came around and I had arranged to go spend the day with Nat in Bournemouth and see some of the sites. It turned out to be a fantastic day out. It was dry and sunny all day and was the only day in January where it didn't rain. An absolute bonus. Bournemouth has a beautiful sandy beach and many attractions and things to do. We spend a very enjoyable hour or so in the Bournemouth Oceanarium and enjoyed a beer and fish & chips at Harry Ramsden's overlooking the beach.

On the Camping and Caravanning Club website it says there are washing machines within one mile of the site entrance but when we asked about it they were not sure where it was at all. I suspect there wasn't at all. Again the Mrs was not happy.

We decided that this was not good at all and with the cost of the electricity it was working out more expensive to stay there than it was on a club site with all the facilities and heated at that. We told the owners we had to move on as I had a meeting in London on Monday and needed to move nearer. This was not entirely untrue just got the wrong day.

So on the Sunday, after being there for only 1 week we moved to the nearest site I could find close to where I needed to be Friday.

Floods.

Having left Black Lion Camping & Caravan Park we had wanted to go to the Chertsey Camping and Caravanning Club site we first visited, mostly because this was very close to where my meeting was on Friday.

I thought it very odd that when I tried to book online it kept coming back with no spaces available so thought best give a ring as there is no way they are full in the middle of January. The recorded message I heard answered that, no they weren't full, they were closed due to flooding. Ah yes of course silly me I should have guessed being right next to the Thames and the news full of reports of the Thames bursting it banks in that area of London

More searching turned up a site in Lingfield, Surrey which is where I spend the first 18 years of my life. It was much further out than I would have liked and would mean an early start on Friday. I gave them a ring and got booked in no trouble for the week.

I was a little concerned as we drove towards the site and had to navigate through a partially flooded road just before turning into the site itself. The drive to reception and on to the pitches was all uphill which felt a bit better, just had the worry about getting out on Friday.

Long Acres Caravan & Camping Park was a vast improvement on the last one. Electric was included, the showers, whilst costing 50p for several minutes, were hot, the facilities were clean and tidy. It's in a beautiful rural location with the Surrey country side all around and offers some fantastic walking.

It is here we began to realise there are a lot more people that live in motorhomes and caravans than you think. There were several people on the site which looked like they had been there a while. A couple of guys we spoke to were builders and move around the country wherever the work is.

The site is directly under the flight path for Gatwick and low aircraft go over every few minutes for portions of the day and night. This did not bother me in the slightest as I lived under that very same flight path throughout my childhood and even after this long time I didn't really notice them except when watching TV. Not because of the noise but it messed up the picture for a brief moment. Now that was annoying.

A few miles up the road is the village of Lingfield where I had grown up and spend many hours fishing tadpoles and all manner of other small aquatic creatures out of the village pond. The same pond that local folk law says the local policeman was thrown in by the "Lingfield Bike Boys" when he tried to interfere with their activities.

Lingfield is home to the Greyhound public house. A beautiful 17th century inn that was my regular and where I enjoyed my first pint of real ale, before I was old enough of course. Directly across the road is the Old Cage Public House that used to be a hotel and restaurant and where my grandmother used to be the pastry and cake chef for many years.

Whilst the village has changed such a lot since those happy tare away days it still has the old oak tree and "The Cage" which was used as the village prison and was last used in 1882 to hold a poacher.

My old secondary school is gone in favour of housing and worst of all the local cafe is now a beauty salon. It's in this cafe, where my grandmother worked after retiring, where I spent many hours being watched over by the notorious biker gang who would give me sixpences to play the pinball machine. Lingfield was a very safe place to live in those days. Not only did everyone know everyone (not always a good thing when you were up to mischief) but the bikers kept any unwanted outsiders away.

Thursday came and it poured down most of the day and all night. Come early Friday morning when we had to leave I was wondering if we were going to be flooded in. I took one of the girls for a walk down to the road to see if we were going to be able to get out.

Before we even got as far the main road itself the bottom end of the drive was underwater where a stream that flowed under it, didn't any more. It flowed over it. Not to be defeated I thought I best see how deep it was. I was well kitted out with waterproof trousers, boots and gaiters so I wasn't about to get wet feet. The dog on the other hand, well, let's say she was slightly less than impressed about wading nearly up to her belly in cold water. The road was still passible beyond the little flood so back we went to start packing up. This is the very last time I ever pack up in the dark, wet and cold. A truly unpleasant experience NEVER to be repeated.

Having got to my clients for my meeting, they had cleared their small staff car park so that I could park my 7.2 meter beast in there, bless them.

That weekend was my weekend to have my 14 year old son, Jacob, for the weekend so after the meeting we drove back to Crawley to pick him up.

Just before we started on our adventures we had popped up to our local pub, The Prince Albert in Copthorne Villiage, for a meal. Mostly because Ann had sold our cooker and we didn't have anything to cook on in the house. We, well she, could have done it in the Motorhome but thought stuff it let's treat ourselves. Whilst there I had a chat to the landlord about stopping in his car park overnight from time to time. He was very happy for us to do so anytime.

With this in mind on Saturday morning we parked up there and got settled in. A trip to the picture house was planned for the afternoon for myself and Jacob whilst Ann stayed with the dogs.

We enjoyed an excellent Sunday roast in the pub (I can highly recommend it). After we had finished the dogs were fetched from the van and brought into the pub with their food bowls so they could finish up what we all couldn't eat.

The pub carpark is very small but the landlord is very welcoming and happy to host 1 or 2 motorhomes overnight. So do please pay him a visit and tell him Gary & Ann sent you.

Dorset.

Our next stop was to find us in Dorset at Shamba Holidays just north of Bournemouth. All the pitches were grass and completely water logged after the prolonged rain so they had us park on the gravel road that ran between the pitches. This was not an issue as there was only one other motorhome on the site along with several caravans dotted around the site all of which are seasonal and unoccupied at the time.

The following morning our only neighbour moved on leaving us alone with six staff to look after us. It was like this for four days where some other motorhomes turned up along with a few of the seasonal residents bringing with them some much improved weather which was set to continue improving over the weekend. At long last, I am really starting to get bored now with the wet and the wind and so looking forward to next winter and NOT being in the UK.

It had an indoor swimming pool with a sliding roof to make it an outdoor pool when the weather permits. A large club house, open only Friday and Saturday during low season, where a good range of food is available to eat in or take away.

I had arranged to pick up Nat from his halls of residence at Bournemouth on Saturday morning for a day out and to explore a local attraction or two maybe.

Since I am a great fan of steam trains I opted to visit Swanage Railway which was about an hours drive away. The railway, unusually, runs all year round but only on weekends during the winter months, between Swanage and Norden. A google map check revealed there was a large parking area at both ends and seeing as you had to pass Norden to get to Swanage this is where we headed for.

Norden is for cars only with signs telling you No caravans and unsuitable for large motorhomes. Oh well, never mind, on to Swanage where, what is called, the main beach long stay car park has 10 or more long bays supposedly for coaches only for just £4 for 24 hours. Now the odd thing is it also says no overnight parking. So having paid for 24 hours, I am not allowed to stay there for 24 hours. How the hell does that work and is that actually legal?

We left Ann in the van with the two dogs and set off to find the station. There was a serious lack of signage in the car park so we had to guess. Not too difficult as the blow of a whistle and a plume of steam rising in the air gave us a clue to the direction.

Having managed to only just miss the train, which was leaving nearly 10 minutes late, we had an hour to wait and grabbed a drink and a bacon roll in the cafe set in an old pullman carriage permanently situated at the end of the platform.

A carful examination of the timetable reveals we have a choice of a two hour wait either at Corfe Castle or Norden where there is a mineral and mining museum. We opted to stop at Corfe Castle as this seemed to be possibly the most interesting and has more to do there.

The journey to the castle, under a perfect blue sky, was a mere twenty minutes and passed through some beautiful views and landscapes. We also passed a camp site with several hard standings almost right next to the track and I made a mental note that next time we are in the area its right there we must stay so I can sit out in the sun and wave at the trains as they pass, very Railway Children. Ann is not really convinced and not keen (Women really just don't get it).

The village sitting below Corfe Castle is a beautiful little village and has a long history with evidence of a settlement around 6000 BC. There is a tiny free museum, the smallest I have ever seen, with various artefacts found in the area to bear this out as well as some recovered rocks with dinosaur foot prints in them. There are also a couple of pubs, hotel, post office, souvenir shop and church.

The castle itself, very impressively overlooks this village high up on the hill and is now owned by the National Trust. The walk up the hill to the castle is roughly paved and moderately steep but well worth the effor,t as once up there you have some amazing views of the surrounding countryside and down to the village.

We rejoined the train and continued on to Norden passing round the castle which towered over us up on the hill and can easily imagine how imposing it would have been in its day. To be honest, it still is very imposing and impressive.

After a brief pause at Norden the train headed back to Swanage. The car park on our return was nearly full and had 4 other motorhomes in the coach bays. Ann told me at one point there were about 10 of them, so seems a popular parking spot for us motor-homers.

Hurricanes.

Because my business partner lives in Kent, we went to Canterbury Camping and Caravanning Club. From there, you can explore the historic town of Canterbury. It's located two miles outside the city but there is a regular bus service to and from the centre just outside the site. The site has an excellent dog walk, although it was somewhat muddy while we were there due to the amount of rainfall there had been over the last month or so.

As well as the famous Canterbury Cathedral you will find wide and varied shopping, museums, attractions and places to eat and drink. I thought the entrance fee to the cathedral a little expensive at £10.50 and that's without a tour. The cathedral is impressive though and was originally built in 597AD and completely rebuilt in 1070 after a major fire destroyed the original.

Within the city, there are some beautiful buildings dating back to the 17th century the most interesting is Sir John Boys House also known as the Crooked House which can be found in Palace Street. It's aptly named Crooked House as it leans and quite an angle with the door and windows leaning over.

I had intended to also visit The Canterbury Tales attraction which, I understand, is an interactive adventure bringing to life the famous tales of Chaucer. And I nearly did until when trying to enter the place via the exit (I have no idea why) I managed to crush my finger in a slamming door which was excruciatingly painful and quickly became very swollen. After that I couldn't be arsed.

When we first decided to live full-time in a motorhome I made the decision to stay in the UK for the rest of the winter to experience it in a "as bad as it gets" kind of way. Little was I to know at the time that mother nature was to decide to teach me a lesson for what I said. It was the time of the 2014 hurricane and our pitch was ideally suited to catch the high winds side on as they raced up the slope towards us. I spent the best part of the night staring up at the dark ceiling where the rear skylight was, with its blind across, waiting for it to suddenly be, not dark. My darling wife on the other hand was expecting us to be overturned at any moment, which is something I really didn't believe could happen.

The winds also forced us to change our plans a little and we stayed on at Canterbury for a few extra days as I refused to drive in winds with 80 mph gusts. The thought of driving along a road and suddenly finding my self in another lane without my say so just didn't appeal to me.

Deserted.

Back in December, my eldest son, Nat, said he wanted to go to the Big Bang Fair next year in March. We went to the fair last year at the Excel Centre in London and was an excellent, fun and useful day out, so I readily agreed.

The 2014 event was to be held at the NEC in Birmingham, which turned out much more convenient as I knew I would be full timing by then and will be easier to get to. With this in mind I did a search for somewhere we could camp within easy reach of the NEC.

I found The Hollies a Camping and Caravanning Club (CCC) Certified Site (CS). A CS is a small campsite that accepts just five caravans or motorhomes and seems to be on small piece of land on a small holding for the exclusive use of CCC members. Probably a good way for the owner of the land to make some extra money from his land and to my mind with little to no effort. I rang them up the other side of Christmas and got ourselves booked in for two nights in March.

March came round quite quickly and we picked up both my sons, after the youngest has finished school, and off we headed north to Birmingham. Now bearing in mind it's a Friday late afternoon just after the weather has improved after a particularly unpleasant, wet, winter and this weekend was also looking to be good. It should have come as no surprise that the M25 was not going to be kind to us.

Once we had got round the M25 and on to the M40 heading north a quick check of the sat-nav confirmed we were going to be much later than expected. So Ann gives them a ring to let them know. No answer, just an answer phone. Ten minutes later she rings again. Still no one there. After a few more attempts Ann leaves a message for them in the hope they do check their messages. I begin to get a sense of "this is not going to go well" especially since after our first experience of CSs.

We finally reach our destination at 7:30 in the evening to find it all locked up and the house certainly appeared to be completely deserted. I maked a few attempts to raise anyone if they are in there but to be honest I knew there wasn't by the way the place looked and the unanswered phone and message.

Despite being somewhat annoyed by this, it did mean I was able to put one of my emergency plans in to action to see how we coped. Now that is really a grandiose name for something not that clever but was glad that I had this all pre-thought out.

First part of the plan is always in place and involves that whenever we leave a site, the grey and black waste tanks are empty (grey is the water from the sinks and black is the toilet waste) and the fresh water tank is full. Well it will be half full when we get anywhere as we lose half a tank when traveling as it slops out through the breather pipe and I will come back to this and how we solved it later.

Part two of the plan involves using an app I have on my iPhone, All Motorhome Parkings – Campercontact to find the nearest place we can wild camp at. Turns out just down the road there is a Toby Carvery listed as being able to take up to 10 motorhomes. I give them a quick call to check they have a place and are still accepting overnight stopovers.

On arrival, as instructed on the phone, I find the manager and she tells me where I have already parked is absolutely fine and confirms they are happy for us to park overnight and would prefer us to eat that evening in the restaurant. No problem I had intended to anyway as it's now a little late in the day due to our delays.

Having had a very nice and inexpensive meal we head back to our motorhome to get set up for the night. This was quite a learning curve as this is the first time we are sleeping a maximum 6, myself, Ann my two sons and the two dogs. This meant having to set up the bed in the middle lounge as a single for the first time as there was no way the two boys were going to share a bed. A lot of bumping around and getting into each others way, no matter how hard you tried to stay out the way, we got all the sleeping arrangements sorted. I think the one most pleased about this was Ellie. Once she realises she gets to sleep on a nice soft quilt with Jacob she looked very happy indeed. It's worth pointing out here that Ellie absolutely adores Jacob and has some special bond with him.

The following morning I pulled a bit of a fast one and offered to take the dogs out of the way while everyone else got organised and put everything away. Smart move on my part I think.

After a brilliant day at the fair Nat leaves us to head for the train station and back to Uni. Now that leaves us to find another place to park up overnight. I had a look on the Camping & Caravanning Club app to find a site about halfway between the NEC and Crawley where I had to drop Jacob off the following day and found the Oxford site to be perfectly situated. A quick ring and were all booked in.

We had a little trouble finding the site, but that was mostly due to the fact that both Ann and myself missed the signs to the entrance on both sides of the road. So we had a nice little detour through Oxford and back round to try again.

This was a brief overnight stop, again not on a pitch as they were all still waterlogged. We shall be returning to this site again later where we will get a chance to stay a few days.

A long stopover.

Briarfields Touring Park in Cheltenham is a site we will keep returning to and to be considered by us as our home site. This is mostly for two very good reasons. Firstly, it's situated perfectly between Gloucester and Cheltenham where we have family in both places. Secondly we very much like the site.

Scott & Jo run a great, very well organised site which seems to be constantly being improved. When we first stayed, the Wi-Fi available was free of charge but could be a little flaky at times. Since then, they have improved it greatly and is now fairly stable, fast and still free.

There is a very regular bus service that runs between Cheltenham and Gloucester and the stop is just outside the entrance so which ever direction you want to go it's no problem. Just down the road and under an underpass, there is a Harvester and a KFC and a little further on is Asda and a few other useful shops like B & Q. You will get a nice detailed map of all this on your arrival.

There is plenty to do in the area and I particularly enjoyed the Gloucestershire and Warwickshire Steam Railway (GWR) which has ample parking and access right next to Cheltenham Race Course with room enough for Motorhomes to park.

It's a good long run with several stops and things to do at each stop if you want to get a full day out. Or, as we did, stay on the train and enjoy the buffet service they offer. This was made extra special for me as I was able to share this experience with my three grandchildren.

Cheltenham is promoted as "The cultural centre for the Cotswolds" and has a bewildering array of museums, galleries, gardens, restaurants and shopping. Oh and of course the famous Cheltenham racecourse home of the Cheltenham Gold Cup. They also host an array of festivals dedicated to the arts throughout the year.

One of the museums I visited was the Holst Birthplace Museum where Gustav Holst, composer of The Planets was born in 1874. His story and that of his music are told alongside a fascinating display of personal belongings in a fine period house showing the upstairs downstairs way of life in his time. It also includes a working kitchen where you can enjoy freshly baked scones.

Just a down the road from the site, in the direction of Gloucester, there is the Jet Age Museum which whilst quite small at present and has a lovely collection of early Jet aircraft such as the Gloster on display and a Vulcan B2 Bomber cockpit still in its original condition (well almost) that you can go and sit in and are told all about the history of this particular aircraft by the very knowledgeable and enthusiastic volunteers there.

Entrance to the museum is free relying on peoples donations and a lovely little cafe that serve hot and cold snacks and drinks. Parking is free and even has parking for your light aircraft should you wish to drop in by plane.

For Harry Potter fans Gloucester Cathedral is a must visit as this is where some of the scenes for Hogwarts were filmed. As you enter the cloisters, it is immediately recognisable as Hogwarts. You can wonder around at your leisure or join a tour. The guides on duty are very friendly and helpful but not pushy at all and if you want to know anything just ask one of them.

Harry Potter aside the Cathedral has a long history dating back to 678 AD when a religious house was founded on the site. It has impressive architecture and stone masonry. King Edward II's tomb can be found within these impressive walls along with 400 other memorials and monuments.

Whilst you're visiting Gloucester it's worth visiting the Gloucester Waterways Museum in the heart of the historic Gloucester docks. It's a wonderful museum with lots of hands on exhibits and great for children of all ages, even the old ones like me. I had a great time here trying out the different block and tackle combinations, feeling the weight of the ropes and seeing how canals worked and were constructed. There is also a narrowboat and a steam dredger moored outside that can be boarded.

The docks still have the old warehouse buildings all around but have long since been converted into other uses. They are none the less still impressive buildings and you get a good feeling of what it might have been like as a busy port.

We stayed at Briarfields for three weeks, which is the longest we have ever stayed on a site so far and I have to admit after two weeks I was ready and itching to move on. It certainly appears I have the travel bug or wander lust or whatever you should call it really bad and not keen to settle in one place for too long. Which is very weird as I have always been the worst one to want to move house in the past even refusing point blank to consider a move let alone look at the possibility. In fact even being a way from home for two weeks on holiday was a strain and so glad to be back home.

Now that I don't have a home, well I do, it's on wheels, so let's say now I don't have a house to return to I don't miss it one bit. In fact, I reel at the thought of returning to living in a fixed location again. I am enjoying living as a full timer and moving on every couple of weeks to new and exciting places.

Tea in Cardiff.

I asked my youngest son, Jacob, where he wanted to go for the Easter holidays and quick as a flash he said Wales. Now this caught me totally off guard, not that he said Wales but his speed of response, it was so unlike him. So I just said "Okay Wales it is." It never occurred to me to ask why Wales.

I did some research as to where we could go and after some searching I came across a site that was right in the heart of Cardiff. Brilliant I thought there is a lot to do there and it's a lovely city so I went and got it all booked.

We picked him up from his mums at the start of the holiday and as we headed out towards Wales it occurred to me I have no idea why he wanted to go to Wales. To see the sheep he said. The sheep, oh dear, were not going to see many sheep in Cardiff. Whoops maybe I should have asked before now. So once over the Severn bridge I made as much a point as I could by pointing out any flocks I could see, but it wasn't many.

Cardiff Caravan Park is a hidden gem in that it's located right in the middle of Cardiff itself, situated within a large multi purpose park, rather like Central Park in New York, although not square, or Hyde Park in London. Whilst the pitch fees are quite expensive the location makes up for this and certainly seems very popular as when we stayed here at the beginning of April the site was just over half full.

The site is very easy to find with good instructions on their website (do note the post code to use for your sat nav and not the address one) and is also very well signposted with the familiar brown signs.

Because it's so close to the city and is not a secure site you need to be a little more security conscious. For example, if you have bicycles on the back of your motorhome make sure they are secured and locked up.

It has a very well established tree and shrubbery line right around the camping area which serves very well to significantly reduce the noise of the city close by. You could almost believe you're actually out in the country. It's so well hidden that many of the locals are not even aware that it's here. Talking to the Tesco delivery man, who I had to explain on the phone where it was, was amazed having played football just a stones throw away had no idea it was here.

This brings up a very good point. When we are in the UK, we do our shopping online at Tesco and have it delivered to which ever site we are on. Make sure you select a temporary address though otherwise they will deliver it to your home address.

Mobile phone reception is very good across all networks, but alas there is no site wifi or public hot spot close enough. There are a number of shops and pubs within 5 minutes walk away with just about everything you could possibly need.

The city centre is just a short 10 to 15 minute walk through Bute Park and comes out right next to the castle. Just over the road from the Castle is the shopping area which contains a mix of high street type shops, victorian style shopping arcades and modern malls.

Cardiff Castle is well worth a visit with its 2,000 year history dating back to the Romans and the reign of Emperor Nero. It's history as a strategically important site, thanks to the River Taff and the Bristol Channel, continues throughout the ages and its thick solid walls even provided shelter to people during the air raids of the Second World War.

For a few extra pounds you can join the 50 minute House Tour which is well worth it. The guide we had was excellent and told us many fascinating stories as we walked through sections of the house that were not accessible to the general public.

For those who love their tea, I can highly recommend Barker Tea house in the high street arcade just off the high street which is the road directly opposite the entrance to Cardiff Castle. They have a bewildering array of speciality teas and hot chocolates along with some very delicious looking home made cakes and serves breakfast between 8:30 and 12:00. After that they serve the traditional cream teas with scones and cakes beautifully presented on a cake tower.

The décor, at first glance, appears to be just old random things but as you sit and look you get the feel that it does have a theme of a Victorian railway station. I may of course be wrong and someone will have a better idea. Either way the seating is comfortable and luxurious with big leather chairs and sofas. A truly pleasant environment to take a break from shopping or sightseeing and meet up with friends for a natter and recharge of the old batteries.

Jacob and myself returned here several times over the fortnight we were here to try the various teas which were served by the pot for one, with proper china cups.

Another absolute must for breakfast is Garlands Eatery & Coffee House found in the Duke Street arcade. They do a marvellous breakfast called a Full Meaty which I can highly recommend. It has everything you need to set you up for a sightseeing or shopping day, well presented, tasty and served on piping hot plates, something that seems to be so rare nowadays.

Cardiff also has one of those huge indoor markets which housed a very special treat for me. On the balcony above the butchers, there is a traditional barber shop, really should be called Sweeny Todd's. They do a Hot Towel shaves for just £13. If any of you guys, or bearded ladies, have never had a hot towel shave now is your chance. Unfortunately this is a dying art form and one of the greatest pleasures that a chap can have. Those that have had them will know what I mean.

A short walk from the caravan site in the same direction of the castle and city centre you can catch the water bus that takes you into Cardiff Bay that has a massive array of restaurants and attractions. Do ask where your stop is to get off, as having read the water bus map. I thought I was being clever and knew where it would stop. Seems I know nothing as we sailed right past it and then had to go all the way around the bus route to get back to the stop before the one we should have got off. The captain was very nice to us and didn't charge any more. It was delightful to sail all around the bay though.

For Dr Who fans, and who isn't, the Dr Who Experience is a must go and see. It's £15 for adults and £11 for children. For your money you get a half hour interactive experience which is very well produced (I would expect nothing less from the BBC) where you have to help the Doctor escape from the Pandorica 2 and along the way in good old Dr Who fashion your put in mortal danger and held captive by the Daleks.

Once you have helped the Doctor escape and got out with your life, you then go into the exhibition area where they have all the costumes of the past Doctors and their companions as well as many props used in the programs.

Huskies.

We spent a week at Ty Mawr holiday park as part of a privately organised camp for Husky owners. Ty Mawr is a large holiday park consisting of static caravans which can be let for a short break or purchased for the more regular visitor. They also have a touring field with EHU and a camping field.

We arrived on a Friday and after booking in and being told we can take any pitch we want within "The Meadows" (the touring field) we pulled into the field and headed for a good spot near the toilet and shower blocks. As we approached and noticed the big Portaloo slogans across the small cluster of buildings. Visions of rock concerts and filthy, smelly toilets filled my head and the thought of "this is not going to be good, and were here for a flipping week". Never mind we have everything we need on board just be handy to be close to a tap has we are going to need to fill up with water a lot more often. So we moved quick smart like to a pitch within reach of a tap but away from the Portaloos.

On the third day Ann decided to venture over to the toilet blocks to have a look anyway and came back having showered to report that the ladies showers were clean and warm. Maybe so I said but I bet the mens ain't. Next day, I buckle out of curiosity and venture over to be pleasantly surprised to find them warm and clean. The showers are well laid out with your own changing cubicle and a shower cubicle within. Small but quite nice and the temperature of the water is controlled by you, another bonus. Goes to show, you shouldn't assume.

In the leaflets, we got on arriving, giving details of all the activities and events going on in the park they boast "Park Wide Super Fast Wi-Fi". Park wide it is, well when it's working, which seems to be a bit random. Fast it is NOT, in fact nowhere near quite quick even let alone super fast. Although it is usable very early in the morning but that's probably because I am the only one using it.

The site has a good range of activities during the day and evening but I cannot comment on these as we spent all our time with the other Husky owners and the activities they organised. It was great to see our two girls mixing and having fun with so many of their own breed and feel they enjoyed the week way more than us.

The most amusing moment for me was as we walked a large pack of about 20+ dogs through the caravan park on the other side of the road, to access the beach. Quite a lot of people came out to watch us pass. It must have been quite a sight for them.

Rally.

When we first got our motorhome I started to get involved with a couple of the forums dedicated to motorhomes. One of which is Motorhome Facts. It so happened that at the time there was a thread that had just started with someone trying to organise a rally dedicated to a legend known as Uncle Norm in East Yorkshire combined with a music meet up. I hope that one day after I am gone someone does this for me.

We drove from North Wales to the Croft Working Mens Club just outside Darlington in Yorkshire and on arrival we were given a very warm welcome by the rally marshals.

Everyone was very friendly and welcoming to us rally virgins and a little ice breaker of a quiz to be played over the next few days certainly helped in getting people out of the vans and wandering around introducing themselves. The site itself was set behind the Club on their field which is right next to the river Tees and temporary EHU was set up for us all. Apparently the toilets on the site were grim so I didn't even go look for myself.

For the first evening we all sat round in a large circle and shared a large cow pie that was made for us all by one of the group and three of the guys brought out guitars and treated us to an evening of jamming with a whole load of very well know and popular songs we could all sing along too. Whilst it was not a particularly warm evening it was a beautiful clear and sunny evening and warm blankets and coats beat the cold.

Saturday we had a motorhome boot sale (like a car boot sale but with motorhomes) which turned out to be very useful for yours truly although it did end up costing me nearly three hundred quid. I brought some Ratchet Tie Down Straps, an awning room and arranged for Jeremy (the owner) to make me up some skirts to stop the girls from crawling under the van. Since he was based a few miles away in Leeds, we arranged to pick them up from him, very conveniently, on our journey back down south on the Wednesday.

Sunday evening was spent socialising, drawing the raffle and a musical feast put together for us from a band that was formed over the weekend especially to entertain us all. The bank holiday Monday saw some of our number leave and head for home or whatever their next destination is. The ones of us left had a bit of a social gathering in the evening with a few drinks and nibbles.

During the weekend, I did ask around to find out if all rallies were like this or was this an exceptionally good one. It seems no two rallies are the same. Each one offering its own mixture of what people want. Some are very social and active like this one whilst others are where everyone stays in their vans and don't talk to one another. Not quite sure the point of the latter one other than a very cheap few days?

Personally I felt the rally was made as good as it was because of the organisers and marshals that ran everything. They went to great effort to ensure there were things we could do as a group and made sure everyone knew about them but no one felt they had to take part if they didn't want to.

On our trek south as well as collecting the awning room we stopped off at Autogas 2000 Leisure Ltd in Thirsk to have our two propane gas bottles replaced with two refillable LPG bottles with an outside filling point ready for when we go over to the continent.

The chap that did our conversion was very friendly and did the job in an hour. He then took me over to where they have a gas pump and showed me how to fill the tanks. The cost to fill both tanks from empty was just £14.40 which is quite a saving from £21.99 X 2 for the Calor bottles and that's if you buy directly from them. Anywhere else will have an additional mark up.

The cost to have the system fitted was £455 so it will take just 15 complete fill ups to recoup my initial outlay, which I have to be honest, is a lot less than I expected. The two other reasons for doing this are 1. I don't have to wait for a bottle to completely empty before I can change it. I can just top it up whenever I get the chance. But mostly 2. finding English Calor bottles over on the continent is like looking for pixies at the end of your garden. Your damn sure they are there somewhere but never seem to find one.

Once done we headed to Boroughbridge Camping and Caravanning Club site for a one night stop. We found them very welcoming and helpful and since Ann is a blue badge holder we were parked on a very convenient hard standing with full service facilities right next to the amenities block. This gave Ann a chance to catch up with getting two of my onesies washed and dried. Good thing as I am down to the one I'm wearing and there is no way that's coming off until I have another to wear....

The onesie dance.

Talking of onesies have you ever tried to put a onesie on without any part of it touching the floor? Well I have and it can be done, but not without a very complex dance and falling into the wall several times as your balance is lost. I am working on perfecting this so no wall support is required, but it's hard.

We were staying at Oxford Camping & Caravanning club site. It's an old site and in need of refurbishment that is unlikely to happen in the foreseeable future and not without good reason. Go Outdoors, who acquired the site 5 years ago, were going to develop the site into a super modern new camp site but for reasons unknown changed their mind at the last minute. On top of this the sublease to the club has not been renewed and has been operating on an annual license ever since. This makes it unwise for the club to invest in major refurbishment if they could be out when the current year is up.

Having said that John and Carol do their very best to keep it clean, tidy and fully operational and in my view they are doing a sterling job and should be congratulated on how well they are doing. The showers are clean and warm but alas the floor in the cubicles get very wet hence my development of the "onesie dance". Once I have this perfected I shall be Trade Marking it and selling licenses to use it.

Our stopover is to be a short one, just two nights, and is mainly for the purpose for stocking up on a few essentials (pegs, walking boots, that special bog roll etc.) from Go Outdoors which is right on the doorstep of the site and it is also a convenient break in our long drive south.

Once all stocked up we went on to spend the weekend at Thriftwood Holiday Park with my youngest son Jacob. Having arrived and received a very warm and friendly welcome we were shown to an almost level hard standing and for only the second time ever I needed to get the ramps out. Other than the fact the pitch was not quite level it did have its own EHU and water supply which I consider a bit of a bonus as makes life a little easier.

We then set up the new Awning Room, we picked up from Leeds a few days ago. It had all been explained to me in detail including cutting the slots in the main panel to feed the ratchet straps in at the same time to keep everything nice and stable.

Well it all took a bit longer than I expected and was awfully glad I had bought rock pegs from Go Outdoors and not just grass ones. I worked up quite a sweat banging all those pegs in. Some more than once as we quickly learned where not to put them and had to make adjustments so the sides were straight (well straightish anyway). Despite fiddling around quite a bit, it still doesn't look as perfect as Jeremy had his at the rally last week. I suppose with practice we will get better at it, oh and faster.

Once all put up to my, almost, satisfaction Jacob and myself set off with the girls for a quick look around the site. It's set in some beautiful countryside and they appear to be doing some further development of new hard standings. We then came across the swimming pool, which was quite frankly, a disappointment being very small and not nice good. The site also seems to be dedicated mostly to static vans and seasonal pitches with just a few touring pitches.

 They have a great dog walk that is well marked out through some lovely woodlands with some fairly steep up and down bits. With two pulling dogs doing the ups is an absolute breeze. However, being pulled down a steep slope involves lots of shouting and colour changes in the trouser department. Dogs loved it though.

You need to have a key to get into the showers which is odd as the nearest village is 3 miles away and the entrance to the site is gated. It's a bloody nuisance as I get all the way to the showers to have to go back and get the key.

Problems Sorted.

We headed back to Briarfields Touring Park for the next couple of weeks as its nice and convenient for visiting the kids and grandkids and we like the place and the lovely couple, Scott and Jo, that own it.

The new awning room was put up in quick time and we were very pleased with it giving us so much more room and the girls can spend as much time as they like out there rather than being all cooped up inside if it's raining.

However, theres a catch which occurred to me early this morning. If were sited on a pitch out of reach of a tap to keep the fresh water tank topped up were going to have to take it all down every few days just to do a service. Damn! That's going to be a serious pain in the what-sit.

To solve this I searched online to source a 12 volt submersible pump which I managed to do so from Amazon, as well as some plastic tubing, a lighter socket and a Hella plug to standard lighter converter. It turned out the very convenient 12 volt outlet close to the water inlet the nice salesman pointed out to me very quickly is not a standard lighter socket but some foreign jobby that is apparently called a Hella plug/socket thing.

My step son James asked if there were anything we need done while we are here so I asked him if he wanted to fit a one way breather to the water tank overflow pipe so we don't lose half a flaming tank of water every time we move.

He did a little more research into this than I had and worked out the best approach is to attach a hose from the overflow out to the side of the van with a tap that can be shut off for traveling and opened again for filling and when parked up as it may also act as a breather for the tank/pump.

Being on a roll for solving problems I had another thought over the issue of my MacBook Pro refusing to charge off the habitation batteries and tried the 12v socket in the rear lounge which has the TV permanently plugged into it. The missus was out getting herself a new hair do so I was safe to unplug the TV without any sharp pains just behind the ear. Ah ha good news it only flipping works. So problem solved. Except that I now have the problem of what happens when I need to use the socket with the TV plugged in. I just have to hope if I get a double socket it will still charge the MacBook.

Flat Tyre.

Having picked up Jacob one Friday afternoon for half term we headed off to Folkestone Camping and Caravanning Club Site. The sat-nav did its usual fine job of getting us to and through Folkstone. It then instructed me to turn down a very narrow road going steeply upwards with a big "PRIVATE PROPERTY" sign at the entrance and also at the bottom of the sign it states "No Caravans Past the Point".

I was seriously confused as I was sure this is the right road but yet, it clearly is not. Whilst sitting there blocking the whole road, dithering and wondering what I am supposed to do now a 4×4 pulls up behind us clearly wanting to go down this road. Well I am no way going to continue with that No Caravan sign as there is no guarantee I will be able to turn round at the other end. So I am going to have to reverse up back onto the main road. However, before that, I get Ann to jump out and go ask the people in the 4X4 behind if this is indeed the road to the campsite, as I was really sure that I am right.

It turns out yes it is. They said follow it down and it's on the right. To say it was steep and narrow is an understatement and it also has some exciting blind corners on it and my doubts begin to creep in again and wondering if the people behind us are roaring with laughter. Oh bugger now there's a car coming towards us. Fortunately they back up to a place we can pass and we carry on until we hit a fork in the road and no flipping sign as to which way to go. So what do I do? I opt to go for the centre of the fork. Duh.

Turns out to be a good move as the 4×4 can then pass to our right stop and tell us to carry on down the right fork and it's just round the corner. I back up a little so I can make the turn and carry on down past a caravan that looks like it's been there a long time with two young foxes hanging around it. They looked very nervously at us but didn't run away and was a rare and nice sight to see such lovely animals that close up.

Having squeezed past our 4×4 friends who had parked on the side of the narrow lane we safely arrived at the Folkestone Camping and Caravanning Club Site where we received the usual warm welcome for a club site and shown to our pitch.

The site is situated on a kind of giant ledge three quarters of the way down the cliffs and in the middle of an area designated of special scientific interest. Behind us, we have the cliffs towering over us and in front and below is the English Channel. Talking to one of the campers here who used to come here in the seventies as a child with his parents said the site hasn't changed one bit, except for a small area at the far end of the site lost to a land slide and the facilities have been updated since then as well.

Dog walking here is amazing. You can easily get down to the beach and sea wall and you have miles of well marked out footpaths and nature trails to explore and all still below the top of the cliffs. Folkestone town centre is only a half hour walk along the coast and a taxi back will cost you £7.50. The only negative I can find with the site is the very large lack of mobile phone signal. I can get a very weak signal from O2 but for the rest there is nothing.

Whilst we were in Cheltenham my step son James came over and fitted a hose pipe to the overflow on the water tank and out to the side of the van and put a tap on the end of it in the hope that we can stop loosing half a tank of water when we travel. Well it worked we arrived with a full tank, brilliant. We also quickly worked out that the overflow is not an overflow, well it is, but as well, it is a breather for the pump so the decision to put a tap that can be opened was a brilliant one. Well done James.

In case you're wondering why I like to travel with all that weight of water on board. It's simply because I like to be prepared to wild camp at any time just in case we either have a problem and are unable to continue without repairs or we simply find somewhere we just have to stop. I have always been one to be prepared, something I learned as a Cub Scout I think.

We suffered our first problem with the Motorhome here. I was on a Skype call. Ann was watching TV and Jacob was outside in the awning doing something, playing on his phone I think, when this very loud noise suddenly starts up quite close to us. Well it sounded quite close.

After a few moments of this Ann goes to investigate and shouts back to me that we have a puncture in the tyre. "WHAT!!!" we have been sited for 5 days now and not moved how the hell can that be possible. I abruptly drop my call "Sorry, problem, got to go" click.

On inspection of said tyre, which was indeed going down, turned out not to be a puncture but even more bizarrely the valve had sprung a leak and air was escaping very noisily. Now was a good time to investigate the spare wheel and the jack I guess.

How you get the spare wheel off is a complete mystery to me as its far from obvious and on top of that the Jack is of the scissor variety supplied with the standard Boxer van and I am in no way brave enough to lift 3.5 tonne with it. I have seen first hand one of these jacks fail, not a pretty sight.

Fortunately my insurance comes with roadside assistance in the UK and throughout Europe so I give the number a ring hoping that roadside assistance also means "on a camp site" assistance. Phew yes it does and someone from the RAC will be with me in approximately an hour. We busy ourselves taking down the awning and clearing all the stuff away from the side of the van so they have a clear working area.

In just over an hour Dave from the RAC turns up and is equally baffled as me as to how a valve can just suddenly go. He says that rather than just change it and leave us to get it repaired somewhere he can get their mobile tyre service to come by in the morning to facilitate a repair on the wheel there and then.

Seeing as we are now on quite a lean and would make somewhat uncomfortable living he jacks it up and uses my ramps under a now completely flat wheel to level it all back up for us. Really nice bloke that Dave.

We go about tidying up and getting everything stacked neatly up next to the van. No point putting the awning up to have to take it down again in the morning. No sooner than everything was all neat and tidy Dave from the RAC calls to say he is on his way back as the tyre man is close by and going to do the job for us now.

Right then let's get this stuff moved "again" away from the side of the van so he can work. Literally just has the last item is moved Dave turns up and starts taking the wheel off and no sooner that was done the mobile tyre unit turns up and replaces the valve, hands it back to Dave and drives off leaving him to put the wheel back on and do the paperwork.

So were all back to normal and the excellent service of the RAC courtesy of our insurance policy has been tested to my satisfaction.

Whoops That's blocked it.

We spent three days wild camping near to where my step daughter lives and works and it was proper wild camping with no EHU no chemical or grey disposal and very limited access to water. How much difference did it make to my normal daily routine? None what so ever!

The solar panel kept the leisure batteries topped up no problem. After the issues I had with charging my MacBook Pro, I found that the 12v outlet in the lounge area that the TV is plugged into, handled the required output with no trouble at all and so this was now no longer an issue. We used gas for heating and cooking. It has been quite warm so didn't need to put the heater on much at all.

We had access to fresh water via an outside tap round the back of the building but was asked not to go round there till after 9 at night so not to be noticed by too many nosey people. This was no big deal as I would pop round there with my very old B&Q orange bucket, fill it up and then pump the water into the tank using the 12v submersible pump I purchased just for this eventuality. So pleased with myself for planning ahead.

The grey waste I was a little bit naughty with and discreetly dumped it in the hedge row close by as I had nowhere else it could go not even a suitable drain. I didn't dump it in the same place twice so not to build up with detergent or whatever and cause any serious issues.

The toilet cassette was another issue and really had to go somewhere proper. So disguising it in a black plastic bin bag I carried up to my step daughters to dump the contents down her toilet. Next thing I know I am up to my elbow in my own excrement trying to unblock her loo with little success. After shoving various implements round the bend include a plastic ladle, a spatula and pouring a bottle of bleach, hot washing up water and some blue chemicals down there (not necessarily in that order) I managed to partially get it unblocked but it was terribly slow to go down with each flush.

A little while later she manages to find a maintenance man who supplied a sink plunger! Well I had a very vigorous go with that for ages and did improve the situation a little and as we waved good bye it still was not right and a specialist was going to have to be called out. Sorry Amanda....

Since having the refillable LPG fitted four weeks ago, we have finally managed to use up one bottle and so now was a good time to have a go at filling it up. We pulled into Pease Pottage service station at the end of the M23 and after identifying where the LPG pump was pulled up alongside whilst trying to remember all the things nice man told me about how to fill it up. I needn't have worried as instructions were clearly displayed on the pump and in terms I could understand. There were pictures.

So I topped up the LPG and looked at the pump display to see how much money I was going to need and promptly headed to the kiosk to pay with the most enormous grin on my face. The poor chap serving me must have thought I had escaped from somewhere as I stand there grinning at him wearing a bright green onesie and paying him the very poultry seven pounds and a few pence. Thats a hell of a lot less that twenty plus quid for Calor bottles.

With that and the fact I now KNOW I don't need to be on EHU even when we stay on sites. Its going to cost an awful lot less to live and that, makes me a very happy bunny indeed.

STOP!

A while back whilst traveling on the Swanage steam railway we passed a camp site and thought that would be one of the coolest places to stay and made a mental note of trying to find it at some point.

Having realised that the rally I had booked to attend months ago was quite close to Corfe Castle which is one of the stops on the railway. I went onto google maps to see if I could find this site. Yeah there it was Woodyhyde campsite. I was straight on the phone to book it. Answer phone. On to the website, filled out the online booking form and hit submit. Two days later I get a reply to say my booking was accepted but also warned me that the entrance to the site was under a low and narrow bridge. I checked my height and width against their "approximate" sizes and we should just fit through. Little did I realise "just" meant within a few millimetres.

The sat-nav took me to the nice, wide, very clearly marked entrance to the track that goes to the site. A few moments after avoiding a dog walker and a minibus speeding towards us we rounded a corner and there it was, the bridge, the very, very narrow bridge and not all that high. I approach it nice and slowly ensuring I am suitable lined up and Ann, sitting next to me is gradually getting louder and louder in her protests that "we are never going to fit" and "I hope you know what you're doing".

"STOP you're going to hit the wing mirrors". She was right. I did, on her side. At this point, I realised I was not as dead centre as I thought I was. Backed up a little to have another go. Got it right this time but part way in CRUNCH I scrape my wing mirror, tiny adjustment left and CRUNCH I scape the other side wing mirror.

It's at this point I realise that a few inches further and the bridge narrows even more. Now here we hit a snag. Having tried a few times in the past to fold the drivers side wing mirror in I have never got it to budge, the passenger side no problem. So I instruct Ann to pull her wing mirror in and I move over to the left by an inch or two.

"STOP"….. Now what. I am now about to hit the retractable awning thingy and rip it off. Ah s*#! I have less than one tenth of a millimetre to spare on my side and it's not finished narrowing. Dammit here goes. I reach out and grab the mirror and pull. Unbelievably our lovely motorhome decides I have done enough damage and I am clearly not going to give up so allows me to pull the mirror in with the greatest of ease. I'm telling you, vehicles are really alive and know what's going on.

Now not being able to see down my side I ease forward, holding my breath and waiting for the sounds of complete devastation and disaster. OMG we are through, We've made it. At this point, I suddenly remembered no one checked if we had enough height. Oh well, must have done. However, we do now sport scratches on both wing mirrors, a bit like battle scars, and should deter anyone from thinking they can take us on.

We turned into the site entrance where a large sign said to pitch up and pay at the shop when it opens. So we located a flattish hard standing close to the railway line (that's why were here, well I am anyway).

We got set up and popped back into the shop when it opened at 5pm. The guy running the place appears to be a bit of a misery but when you get to know him a bit he's alright and quite friendly in his own way. The shop is very well stocked with everything you could need for camping as well as a good selection of food and most importantly beer, wine and local cider. The cost was a very pleasing £8 per night for all of us without EHU.

The nearest village, according to google maps, is a 20 minute walk away but since I was only here for a day and a bit I didn't bother. Anyway I wanted to sit and watch the trains go by with carriages full of children and old people grinning and waving at me like they all know me or something. It was hard not to wave back, so I did, and hope it made their trip on a steam railway that little bit more special. I can be quite nice sometimes.

More disasters.

Following the tyre valve incident and the bridge nightmare we suffer again, but this time it's a double whammy.

We attended a rally organised through Motorhome Fun at Norden Farm and met the most amazing, friendly and helpful people you would ever wish to meet anywhere. Which was very fortunate for us as we really did need friends during the next 10 days.

Norden Farm is a fantastic camp site situated close to Corfe Castle and is a fully working farm with several camping fields of various types many with electric hook ups. The mobile network is a bit on the shaky side offering only 1 or 2 bars on all the networks but does have 3g. WiFi is excellent being provided by Club wifi and offers a range of timed packages and all seem to be unlimited bandwidth and plenty fast enough to stream your favourite TV show. The onsite shop is well stocked with just about everything you would need plus plenty of stuff to care for any horses and other animals you may have brought along. The shower and toilet facilities are very good and there is even a shower room for dogs (this please Ann greatly but don't think the dogs were that happy about it). The site is surrounded by copious public footpaths through woodland and fields in all directions so the walking is brilliant. This is the place where the first of our incidents hit.

I was taking the girls out for their early morning walk along the Purbeck way (one of the marked public footpaths) and was on the return trip close to camp where I managed to turn my ankle badly, just how badly I would discover over the next few hours.

As always I was wearing a good pair of walking boots which helped support my ankle and I was, after a few minutes, able to hobble back to base. Once I had the dogs sorted with water and tied up outside I removed my boots and settled down to get some emails answered.

A short while later I went to get up to finish making my cuppa and thought ouch that hurt and looked down at a foot I didn't recognise it. It had grown quite a large lump on the ankle. Now that can't be good. I examined it closely, Ann examined it closely, Ann went and got someone else to examine it closely, a nurse examined it closely. Everyone except me didn't think it was broken.

My foot was plunged into a bucket of freezing cold water despite my hollering and yelling and made to keep it there for half an hour (which was 29 minutes and 59 seconds longer than I thought was good). We all went through the examinations again and were clear to all that it had swollen more.

I was manhandled into a car and taken to Poole hospital where I sat for the rest of the morning and well past lunchtime while I was seen by triage and the foot was x-rayed and was then told that they cannot see a break so must just be tendon damage. "Just tendon damage" do they have any idea how flipping much it hurts? They strapped it up with a bandage or two and sent me away. I got myself a taxi back to the farm which was not close by. In fact £35 worth of not close by. That hurt nearly as much as my ankle.

I would like to say the next few days of rest went by without incident and I recovered. But I can't. No I spent the following days and nights in very large amounts of pain, not sleeping for long at a time, and generally feeling very miserable for myself. To cheer myself up a little and to have some form of ability to get around the site and take part in, or at least watch, the activities being organised I hired a mobility scooter which two very kind ladies went to collect for me.

Sunday was Ann's birthday and a mass barbecue was organised and she was over the moon to receive cards and a present from all our new friends who we had only just met and had been running around after her fool husband.

Come Tuesday morning I had resigned myself to the fact that I was not going to be walking or driving for a few weeks at least and certainly not by Thursday when we were supposed to be picking up my son Nathaniel from Bournemouth University. I spoke to my ex and enlisted her help in getting him picked up. So we now need to talk to the site owner about staying on for God knows how long.

Ann then says that the van has sunk into the ground and squashed the electric cable with it. Errr no, it's not sunk but we have a flat tyre, again, and yes it's the valve AGAIN, not the same one I hasten to add but the one on the opposite side. I did a google and found Mobile Tyres.net and got them to replace all 4 valves with steel ones to avoid this happening again.

Three weeks later and we are still at Norden Farm. I bought a cast boot and it has helped a great deal and given me some mobility but still can't walk more than a few yards. Poor Ann has had to do everything including emptying the Loo which I keep filling up as I can't make it as far as the loos here.

Norden Farm have been very understanding about the situation and allowed us to stay where we are and if I am still unable to drive by the time the holiday season starts, where they are fully booked, will find us somewhere on site and move the van for us. With my progress, so far I doubt that will happen but still need more time to heal, at least I am now getting sleep at night without waking every 2 hours screaming in agony and able to bear a little weight on the foot.

I had James, my step son, and his friend come down from Cheltenham to camp here for a week, all expenses paid, to help Ann with the chores and to walk the girls who were getting very fed up at not being walked very far.

4 weeks later and we are still at Norden Farm. I have been able to move the van but only to turn it round 90 degrees to avoid having to keep taking the awning down because of the wind which always seems to blow in the same direction

and very hard, probably due to the fact that the site sits in a valley which is perfect for channelling the wind. That and the number of mole hills around our wheels were reaching alarming proportions. We booked in for a further 2 weeks where I will have to be fully fit to drive as we have a UK/Scotland tour planned with my son Jacob during his summer holidays and I calculate we will be running out of LPG by then.

Despite the set back we are still loving the full timers lifestyle and I take the view that if we weren't paying for a pitch here we would be paying for a pitch else where, so not much different other than the view hasn't changed in a while.

North.

For the summer school holidays and just prior to us leaving the country for the first time on our adventure I thought it might be good to experience some of Scotland. I had planned a route that took us up the west side of the country, across the top of Loch Ness and down the east side.

After a particularly long and slow drive up country to the Midlands we arrived at Drayton Manor Camping and Caravanning Club site, our first stop, which is situated right next to Drayton Manor Theme Park. We were given a very friendly and warm welcome and were shown to our pitch which was the usual CC&C hard standing on loose stones and whilst ours was perfectly level I did note that the site was on a gentle slope and so some other pitches were not quite as level.

The entrance to the theme park is just across a car park from the site. It's not the main entrance and when we arrived just after the park opened there were no queues at all.

It's a typical theme park with rides to suit all ages and abilities and with the added benefit of a small zoo. In comparison to Chesington, it seems quite a bit smaller. Despite it being at the beginning of the school summer holidays, a Saturday and a very hot one at that, it was not particularly busy and waiting times for even the big rides were less than 30 minutes so my son Jacob got to ride on everything he wanted. Food was not terribly expensive and two good meals with drinks were less than £14.

The following day we traveled up country on the M6 heading towards our next stop in the Lake District which to me is one of the most beautiful places on earth and as the landscape ahead changed and the mountains begin to rise into the sky I cannot help myself but to smile at the beauty and splendour.

Just before we left the motorway, we came across a motorway service station called Farm Shop. Well worth a stop but be warned, you won't be able to drive away without purchasing some of the most delicious and mouth watering locally produced goodies they have on offer there.

Arriving at our next stop was Troutbeck Camping and Caravanning Club Site. The site is not your traditional C&CC site, it kind of looks like they have taken over a static caravan holiday site and added a good number of hard standings all around it.

The site has a licensed shop which is stocked with all the basics and the showers and toilets are warm and clean. There is a children's play area to keep your little darlings amused for a while at least.

If you are a walker or have dogs then this place is absolutely heaven. Being in the Northern Lake District and at the foot of Blencartha better known as Saddleback, one of the most northerly mountains in The Lakes and rises to a height of 2,848ft (868 meters). The site sits on one of

DEFRA's Conservation walks which is a well sign posted circular walk.

There is a bus stop just half a mile up the lane where the regular bus service between Penrith and Wokington stops and Keswick is just a 15 minute ride away. Alas our visit was quite short and we didn't have time to venture into Keswick.

As we continued on our way north towards Scotland one of those pretty little yellow lights appear on the dashboard, you know the type, the ones that warn you something very expensive is about to happen. This was the one that looks like an engine so thought I had better pull over and find out what it means. Out comes the manual and flicking to the relevant page tells me, it is a "emissions warning" light and tells me I should visit a dealer immediately to have it checked.

A quick Google tells me there is one in Penrith about 20 miles away. We turn up at the dealership totally unannounced and to my amazement they can look at it straight away for me, oh and there is a standard fee of £90 to hook it up to their diagnostic computer. I am so excited that they can do it so quickly I just say yes please.

So the dogs are not upset I stay with the van whilst Ann and Jacob are taken round to the coffee machine. This was not such a great idea as I sat there whilst the mechanic spent, what seemed like hours with his laptop connected to my electrics and the longer he spent the more the feeling of deep foreboding and expense weighed me down.

Eventually he wandered off and returned with the nice lady from reception to break the news to me. It was some kind of valve to do with the emissions system or whatever and they have it in stock and can do it straight away however it will take a few hours. Oh and its £558. No problem I say and dig out my Super duper silver warranty and give it to the nice lady.

Then she says they will run me, the wife, son and 2 dogs into town and pick us up at about 3pm when they have it all done. So I get the dogs out the motorhome and they take me and the dogs in a small van. Ann and Jacob travel in a car into Penrith.

Penrith is an old market town that once used to hold a corn market. The site is still there and now holds a market on a Tuesday but not for corn I am guessing. There is also the ruins of an old castle and the usual array of shops, tea shops and coffee houses.

Whilst we are sitting munching on some sausage and chips from a chippy right by the old market square I get a phone call from the garage to say they have spoken to the warranty company and because that particular part is not listed in the warranty book its not covered. No surprise there then. I don't think I have ever had anything go wrong on a vehicle that IS listed. OK I say do it anyway I'll pay.

After wandering around, drinking coffee, Ann getting her hair done, wandering around some more and buying a few things 3pm finally comes and it starts to rain. Oh joy of joys. We give the garage a call to get them to come and pick us up so we can sit in the dry and drink some more of their coffee and they tell us that they were just doing the paperwork and were about to ring us.

Five minutes later were on our way back to the garage where I get to severely damage my credit card balance and find out they not only were they running us around but cleaning the motorhome for us as well. I have to admit that whilst the £558 hurt I was very pleased with the service we received at David Hayton Ltd, after all we turned up unannounced with what turned out to be a largish issue and were back on the road in about 5 hours as well as looking after our needs very well.

The way I see it. Things will go wrong with your car or your house from time to time anyway. The fact that our car and house are rolled into one makes no difference so something like this does not impact in the least to our newly chosen lifestyle.

Scotland.

I am sorry to say I have finally found a C&CC site that does not live up to the high standards we have been getting used to. Don't get me wrong it's not a complete disaster just not as great as the others we have visited so far.

On arrival at Culzean Castle Camping and Caravanning Club site, we were booked in efficiently (notice I didn't say warmly) and shown to our pitch where, for the first time at a club site, we needed to use the levelling ramps. The surface was not great either, very old and tired looking, and a dirty surface at that, and was in desperate need of some maintenance

The facilities block also looked in need of some renovation although they did keep it relatively clean. The disabled room, which had to double up as a family room, also had a broken shower head but was still useable. The floor was very slippery which is not suitable for a disabled room at all.

The reception had a few bits and pieces for sale such as sweets, ice cream, a few tinned items and milk but I didn't see any bread in there. All this is not a great deal of use really as its only open for 1 hour in the morning and 1 in the afternoon in high season.

It was no surprise to me that because the site is old and tired that the staff are not as happy and proud of it and so do not come across as friendly as we have encountered on other club sites.

The site is just outside of National Trusts Culzean Castle grounds and NOT in it as the intro on the clubs detail page says and to go into the grounds will cost you £15.50 unless you're a National Trust member. Feeling slightly conned I decided I would not part with further money to visit the castle.

The bus stop is just outside the grounds and there is a regular service to Ayr which seems to be the closest big town of the area. Like the site, alas, Ayr is old and tired and I doubt it helped that, on the day we visited, it rained constantly making it feel very drab. The effects of the current economic state are very prevalent there with many shops, closed and boarded up.

On the plus side at the site there is some nice walking through the surrounding forest although I never felt too sure if I was trespassing on private or National trust land as the signs we came across were not very clear as to which bit was private and which wasn't. Since no one shouted at me or tried shooting me I guess I was either alright or simply just got away with it.

Continuing our journey up the west side of Scotland was an amazing geographical treat despite the fact it rained for most of it. We sat in awe and amazement as we passed from the lowlands into the dramatic mountains and lochs of the highlands.

We drove up the west side of Loch Lomand with the Trosach mountains majestically towering around us. Loch

Lomand is the largest of the Scottish Lochs by area and is 36km (22.3 miles) in length, but it did seem much further. Alas every pull in we passed was on our side of the road had trees and bushes blocking the view of the loch so we didn't get the opportunity to stop for a photo or two. I have since been informed by those in the know that I must have missed a few as they are there.

Having eventually got to the top of the loch we continued on north to our destination at Oban Camping and Caravanning Club Site and received a very friendly and warm welcome. The site is not actually near Oban, in fact it is some 13 miles away but there is a regular hourly bus service from right outside the site into Oban operated by the friendliest of bus drivers I have ever encountered.

The site is within the walls of a Victorian walled garden that was originally used to grow pineapples and other exotic fruits for the manor house close by. It later was used to grow more traditional vegetables for the market in nearby Connel before being turned into a caravan park.

Because of the wall all around the site it is well sheltered from any wind. Having said that every so often a sudden gust of wind travels through the site and just as suddenly disappears again. It may have been the ghost of a witch which is said to haunt one of the nearby roads just passing through on her way to scare some weary travellers.

Through the side gate just outside the wall and over a bridge is Sutherlands Grove which is part of the Scottish national parks and has colour coded walks and cycle paths of various circular lengths. The walks are absolutely fantastic and take you through the forest with well marked out trails depending how far you fancy walking and are all graded as moderate walking, I found them very easy going with just a few steep bits. Make sure you have your camera with you as not only is there some beautiful streams running over rocks and a good variety of trees and bushes, we also spotted a deer a couple of times as well.

Oban is a lovely town that has grown up around the very successful Oban Distillery since the late 1700's and has a very impressive range of shops and restaurants. With the local fishing business Oban has become a very popular place for fresh seafood and is recognised as the seafood capital of Scotland.

The distillery right in the centre of the town is well worth a visit where the tour will help you to understand what makes Scottish malt whiskey so very special and the great lengths they go to to keep to the original recipes and processes that makes each malt so special and individual. You will also get to try a very special malt straight from the cask as well as a dram of Oban 14. They will also let you keep the special glass you used in the tasting.

As I write this I am sitting with my special glass with a wee dram of the Distillers Edition Oban malt I purchased in the shop on my way out of the distillery.

Half way.

Just over half way round our Northern England / Scotland tour and the furthest north we are going. I have to admit that I feel I have been spoiled with the easy driving motorways provide, as driving in the highlands has been quite an experience and quite hard work with the many gear changes and the much slower speeds. Don't get me wrong I am not complaining and is no doubt preparing me for our trip down to Spain in four weeks time via France, Belgium, Netherlands, Germany, Switzerland, Italy and France. Well that's kind of the plan but we will see.

Loch Ness Shores Camping and Caravanning Club site is a lovely site situated right next to the loch itself and have a fresh modern feel about it where customer service is important. The shop is open from 9 in the morning until 9 at night and has a great range of easy to cook foods including delicious ready meals supplied by a local butcher. What a contrast to Culzean Castle.

My only issue with the site is its wifi. It's not part of the C&CC wifi system but one run by Highland wifi which seems to be owned by a Dutch company. Whilst not terribly expensive and unlimited bandwidth based on the time you purchase, don't bother, its very slow. If you have a photo you wanted to email to a friend in North Yorkshire, you would be quicker taking your camera to him yourself than waiting for the email to send. All was not lost though as I was able to get a passable 3G signal.

Whilst being in the middle of nowhere there is a local bus service to Inverness that leaves just outside the camp site once every 2 hours during the week and only twice on a Saturday for only £4 return and they run on time.

This is something that has fascinated me since using public transport in Scotland. It's on time, it's very inexpensive and the drivers are really nice people. The complete opposite to down south where I originally come from. I was amazed during my journey to Inverness when the driver on more than one occasion pulled over to allow a car to pass us. Down in southern England, the drivers would rather poke themselves with burning needles in the eye than do that. Scotland has the rural bus service that I remember we had when I was a kid, long may it continue.

Inverness itself is great for shopping and has everything in it, which is no real surprise considering its size, however what was a pleasant surprise was the butchers that is right by the bus stop you get on and off at. It's been there for just over 100 years and is still run the same way as it's always been. With the butchers, and theres a good few of them, not handling any money at all. Instead you take a ticket to take over to the cash desk where you pay there. Just how they was like when we were kids, brilliant.

A couple of months ago we got a call from the GP surgery we had been registered with for the past 10 years. We were told in a somewhat abrupt manner that because we no longer lived in the area we were no longer registered with them and we had to make other arrangements. I explained that we did not have a permanent address and could not register anywhere else. But they already knew this as had given a letter ages ago to use to get repeat medication where ever we went. "You will just have to register as a temporary patient where ever you are then" click and they hung up. Nice.

So whilst we were in Dorset near Corfe Castle we visited the local GP practice and were supplied with one months supply of what we needed. Although I did get the impression the doctor was not entirely happy with this and it was the minimum amount he could give.

As we were approaching the site at Loch Ness, I noticed a medical centre within a short walk of the site and at the first opportunity walked up there to see if I can get some medication. Whilst explaining we were roamers and showing the letter we had to the receptionist the practice manager came over having over heard what I was saying, and asked if I had my medical pack. I gave her one of my completely blank stares (something I am very good at) as I was trying to work out what the hell she was on about and then said "a what?".

It appears that our last surgery, when we left, was supposed to supply us with a medical pack that contained all our medical notes to carry around with us. I laughed and said you got to be joking they didn't even give us a chance to discuss our options and hung up on me. She said she will look into it for me and made an appointment to see the doctor the next day.

I arrived for my appointment in good time and whilst I was waiting the nice practice manager lady came out to speak to me and said she had printed out a pack for me for my medical records but only from today onwards and had given them to the doctor.

The doctor was wonderful and gave me a full exam and took bloods for a complete check and said they would be in by the end of the week and if I came in then they will give me a copy of the results. She also gave me a 2 month supply of all my medication, of which there is quite a lot as I am a hypertensive diabetic (thats a diabetic with high blood pressure), to last me until we go abroad, filled out all the details in a nicely bound set of printed sheets designed for medical notes and then placed it in a blue plastic folder to keep it nice.

I went round with her to the pharmacy (same place as reception) where they photocopied my prescription to include in my notes as the good doctor was not happy with my blood pressure and had increased one of the dosages and wanted me to carry on with the increased dosage but under the strict instruction I was to purchase a BP monitor and keep an eye on my pressure, which I am now doing. It also appears that prescriptions are free in Scotland.

Overall it appears that if you want excellent healthcare you need to go live in a remote part of the Scottish highlands where it seems GP's still actually care about the well being of patients rather than the cost.

Time To Head South.

Having spent a week at the most northerly point we were going, in fact the most northerly point I have ever been, we begin our travels southwards with a plan to reach the most southern point we can in Spain by the beginning of December, 15-16 weeks or there a-bouts. Seems plenty of time but we don't intend to take the most direct route nor are we in a rush, so who knows.

We stopped off for a week at Scone Camping and Caravanning Club site which is a few miles outside Perth but not that easy to get to. The bus stop is a good couple of miles away or you can drive an extra couple of miles to a Park and Ride.

Scone site has a mobile butcher van visit the site twice a week and not only sells local meat but pies, bread and other essentials as well. The lady was very nice to us and on her second visit of the week brought us some chicken carcasses for the dogs. Needless to say they didn't last very long at all.

Scone Palace (Pronounced SKOON and best done in a Scottish accent or it just doesn't sound right) is just across a couple of fields and an easy walk. You go in to the grounds by the back way and so avoid the ticket office at the front which means you can get away with walking round the extensive grounds for free, if you're that way inclined. You will need to go and purchase a ticket if you want to go look inside the palace itself.

The palace and grounds are impressive which should be no surprise given that it has such a colourful history and one of Scotland's most important stately homes. Its fifteen hundred years of history includes the crowning of Macbeth and Robert the Bruce. As well as the extensive collection of antiques, paintings and rare artefacts you can also see a replica of the Stone of Scone otherwise known as the Stone of Destiny steeped in myth, legend and tradition.

Next stop was Lauder Camping and Caravanning Club site in the Borders. It's a very rural site being 4 miles from the town of Lauder and is an hour or so bus ride to Edinburgh.

The bus stop is right down the road and not far to walk at all however the bus only goes, and returns, once every two hours. It is really a little too far from Edinburgh due to the travel time and the fact if you miss the last bus back it will probably be cheaper to buy a car than the cost of a taxi. Having said that though we did venture off to Edinburgh as I wanted to look round Edinburgh Castle.

I was a little concerned that the Castle is in some kind of financial problems as of the two museums within the walls (there are more than two I just couldn't be bothered with any more) I went into had the lights turned right down low. This made it difficult to see the exhibits in any detail. When I pointed this out to my son Jacob he gave me one of those exasperated looks and said "They are low for effect not because they can't afford the electricity."

I have done such a lot of sightseeing since we began our travels and one thing I have begun to realise is that I much prefer to do so when the weather is nice. It wasn't a bad day really and we didn't get rained on, but it was very grey and cold. Because I have the luxury of time and not have to cram in what I can in two weeks of the year I am going to hold off in the future for a better day for sightseeing from now on.

We did enjoy watching the 1 o'clock gun being fired. The L118 Light Gun is fired every day of the week except on a Sunday and is a tradition since 1861 when a 18-pdr cannon was used. It was originally fired to provide ships in the Firth of Forth with an audible time signal to accompany the visual signal of the time-ball dropping at the top of the Nelson Monument. This helped shipping set the maritime clocks needed in order to navigate the globe.

Nudists.

If you ever fancy trying what I consider the best fish and chips EVER then you must visit Barnard Castle camping & caravanning club site. It's not far from Darlington and the fish and chip van visits there twice a week. It's another site in a rural location and the area is great for walking. The girls really loved it there. We only stayed a couple of days so didn't have a chance to really explore the area properly.

Having paid a quick visit to the motorhome service point we began the trek south taking a brief detour out towards Hull to visit Wandahome's accessories superstore. Alas we were somewhat disappointed as it wasn't so much the superstore as a … well, shop I suppose and failed to have all the lovely goodies we were planning on purchasing from them.

So disappointed we continued our journey south towards Copthorne in West Sussex which according to the sat nav it was a five hour drive. So as is becoming the norm I settled in for the drive. The plan was to stop off at some point midway to do a wild camp overnight.

Things didn't go quite to plan. I find it incredibly easy to drive the motorhome and we just ate up the miles and the hours just shot by unbelievably quickly and before we knew it we had reach the M25 and a mere 60 miles from our destination which we were not supposed to be at until the following day. So Ann started making phone calls and rearranging our plans for a day forward which included picking up stuff for my son to drop off to him at his digs at university. We also rang the Prince Albert Pub and let the landlord know that we were coming and to put some dinner up for us. Of course being a mighty fine chap and as we stop off there every time we pass, he did so.

This meant the girls spent the entire day in the motor home bar a couple of quick stops to just have a wee and for me to fuel up with coffee. They were both perfectly behaved and didn't complain once. So having arrived at the Albert, got parked up, nipped off to eat the meal put aside for us I then treated the girls to an extra long walk as they thoroughly deserved it before returning to the pub for a few drinks which, in my opinion, I thoroughly deserved.

The following day we travelled down to Bournemouth to collect my eldest son and deliver his stuff before heading to Southsea Leisure Park for a week. Whilst its location appears to be great, right on the sea front with easy access on to the beach it was a major let down. The site was grim, very tired and unkept and the beach, well, not great. Also a warning, or maybe a tip, there is a nudist section very close by! I am not sure it's an official one as the only mention of it is on the park map you get, and there are none of the usual warning signs. I did wander along to it whilst walking the girls and indeed it is actively used as a nudist beach. Yeah I know but it had to be done, more than once just to be sure.

There is a regular bus service from close to the site that takes you to Portsmouth Historic Dock Yard and I can very highly recommend it for a good day out. The "All Attraction

Pass" is excellent value and includes free water bus over the bay to the two attractions they have over there.

They have a number of excellent attractions all included in the price including the Royal Navy's most famous warship HMS Victory and my favourite the Royal Navy Submarine Museum where you can board the HMS Alliance which is an 'A' class submarine built for service during World War II. The guys on duty there are all ex-submariners and so have first hand knowledge of submarine living and operation.

Whilst we were at Southsea we took the motor home in to Dolphin Motorhomes in Southampton to have the engine and habitation service and the MOT done. I am pleased to say all passed with flying colours. However, they did note that the rear of the vehicle was very close to the bump stops and I was warned we may be overweight on the rear axle. When we got back to the site I proceeded to move everything around so that the heavier items were moved forward and also took this as a chance to throw out anything that has not been used since we moved in. It's now looking much better on the back end.

South of South.

We finally made it over to mainland Europe after spending eight months full timing in the UK.

The journey via the Euro Tunnel went very smoothly and was nice and easy. For those who have not used the Euro Tunnel to get over to France, it's simple. As you arrive you go through what looks like toll booths but are in fact automatic check in booths. If you have pre-booked your ticket your number plate is automatically recognised and a simple press of the screen will print your boarding hanger, to place on your rear view mirror, with a large letter on it, ours was D. You then follow the signs to the coach, caravan and motorhome parking area that has a large display screen which will tell you, by your letter, when to proceed.

We had arrived early for our train so wandered over to the terminal building which was quite like a motorway service station and had some breakfast. I then had plenty of time to try to work out how to fit the beam deflectors to the headlights which a large sign at the entrance to the terminal building had handily reminded me. Thanks to whoever thought of putting that there I had completely forgotten and would probably have never remembered, till I got nicked that is.

Once our number, well letter, had come up with instructions to proceed we followed the big blue signs pointing to France, went through passport control for the UK and passport control for France. Yes that's right 2 borders in a short distance, made me feel like we were going through checkpoint Charlie in the good old days just without all the guns pointing at you. We were then, or maybe before passport control I forget, told to pull over by some special buildings to have our gas checked.

Having satisfied themselves I had turned off the gas (they have to check themselves can't just tell em) we proceeded to boarding the train. Having seen a coach and another motorhome ahead of us disappear into the side of the train I thought can't be that hard and it wasn't. It was just one of those stupid things I was worrying about having had that incident with the bridge in Dorset.

After a short 35 minute train ride we arrived in Calais and drove off the train, out of the station and on to French roads with Ann, my darling wife, constantly repeating to remember to drive on the right. I mean come on just because I got it wrong when we were in Germany ONCE. As it goes about half an hour out of Calais, I got it wrong again, whoops. Boy did she scream at me.

I had programmed the sat nav for a camp site we had been recommended in Brugge, Belgium as our first stop and made sure I had selected the 'No toll' option. This meant we were taken along some quite narrow but empty roads through some farm land and also through some very pleasant French villages of which one we decided to pull over in and grab a coffee from an almost empty bar before popping next door to a Lidl for some bits. As, in the past, my French came flooding back and was able to communicate quite well. It's a funny thing but I can hardly speak a word of it in the UK but as soon as I am in France it just comes spilling out. Not that I know that much but a damn sight more than when in the UK, weird.

Continuing on into Belgium and Brugge to find our campsite, Camping Memling. A lovely site which is quite compact compared to the ones in the UK, seems they don't have the 6 meter rule here, with very friendly staff that speak loads of languages including English. We were later to discover most people in Belgium speak several languages. I did think it is amusing though that there were lots of english words used in shop signs and posters, especially where they had the shop name in Flemish with an english tag line under it. The sign outside the camp site instructing you to park in the street before checking in was only in english, odd.

Bicycles rule in Belgium and as far as I can work out that unless it specifically says so they have right of way over everything including pedestrians. I am guessing that if you knock over a cyclist something very, very bad happens to you. It looked to me that the drivers in cars were petrified of them like they were tyrant rulers or something.

The camp site is situated just two kilometres outside the main city which is a good half hour or so walk, a very regular bus ride or as I decided to do a 5 minute bike ride. It's probably more if you take your time and have to peddle yourself but since I was on a electric bike and I felt like a tyrant ruler I bombed along as fast as it would go. It was rather a strange experience being on a road / cycle path and feeling safe.

The city itself is beautiful having been here since 1000AD. It has a fascinating and very important history and its links with the Medici family which you can learn about at the Historium which can be found in the Markt square in the centre of the city. I highly recommend you visit this as for €11 you can take a very cleverly done interactive tour through several themed rooms which tell Brugge's history through a love story of boy meets girl, boy looses girl, boy finds girl again…….

Now a word of warning. Brugge has a lot of breweries, not as many as it used to have, but still a lot and they make strong beer. That will be lager to the British but they call it beer. Don't bother asking for lager they have no idea what it is neither do they know what bitter or ale is. Having had a local beer with my lunch at a rather quaint restaurant by one of the canals, I wondered into the Beer Museum just round the corner from the Historium.

To be honest, its rubbish, you walk around with an iPad pointing at QR codes, little squares with chunky dots on it, thats by some picture or painting and either listen to or read some stuff that was … well … a bit boring and you get the impression they struggled for material. There were a few interesting bits here and there but not much. When you get bored, it didn't take me long, you go down stairs to the bar where you can choose to try 3 of the 8 or so different beers they have on tap there, you can buy more if you like. It's better if you go as a small group as then you can pool your 3 drinks each and try them all between you as I saw a group doing.

Let me repeat the warning ….. whilst what you get is only 33cl, a third of a litre, by the time your have necked them and added to the beer you had less that an hour previously and remember its strong stuff, you leave there a little light headed and the chocolate shops beckon to you, and there is a lot of them. Of course, you're no longer in a state to resist so you wander in and they don't play fair, they offer you free samples. So after being in 3 or 4 you're not only slightly tipsy and your sugar levels have reached new highs and your feeling just that little bit sick. I now have every sympathy for toddlers who have dodged their parents watchful gaze and gorged out on chocolate and had a try of uncle Georges beer when he wasn't looking at a family gathering. The ride back on the bike was fun though.

Change of plan.

Having spent a lovely week in Brugge, it was time to begin our journey southwards. We thought it would be nice to visit Luxembourg on our way down and spend a week exploring there.

It was on this leg of the trip I was pleased to prove that my plan for "not booking anything but just turn up and decide then" was a good plan. Having arrived at my carefully chosen camp site discovered that I had no mobile signal at all and so was not a suitable stop. We had met a couple in a supermarket car park just 10km up the road who was telling us about an excellent site which as it happens was just a little further down the road with free wifi and a good mobile signal. So we turned round and headed to this site instead.

Camping Bissen is a lovely site where they have touring pitches right next to a river in a gorge which was absolutely beautiful. We had planned to stay here for a week but on closer inspection of the map, calculating the distance we have gone so far and how much further we had to go I decided at this rate we will be very hard pressed to reach Malaga area by December.

I worked out where would be a good point to head to and programmed the sat nav, making sure that toll roads had been deselected. WHAT 8 hours!! So I tried again with toll roads, only 4 hours. So that's it then we are just going to have to use toll roads. Something I didn't want to do as we will miss out on so much but had severely underestimated how much longer it would take us.

We drove out of Luxembourg back into Belgium and then into France where we joined our first toll road. Unfortunately because our motor home is a right hand drive Ann, my darling wife, has to deal with the auto tolls. We pull up to the machine and she hangs out the window with my credit card in hand, looking at the instructions and buttons, which are all in French, and shouting back at me that she doesn't know what to do. Eventually a ticket appears out the machine and the barrier goes up and we were off.

The weather was atrocious when we started and by the time we reached the point to turn off towards my chosen site it hadn't improved one bit so we just kept driving south (again my plan is good). Having pulled over to get something to eat at a service station I selected another site 3 hours further on and headed for that deciding that regardless of weather this is where we will stop.

As we approached our exit from the toll road the weather had begun to improve and it seemed that all was going to be good. Then we reached the automatic toll booths …….

Again with Ann hanging out of the window with the ticket and my credit card there ensued some shouting with me making it very clear, or so I thought, not to put my credit card in anything until the price was known, my credit card being shoved in any slot it would fit first. A man's voice coming through a speaker saying something in french and before I can instruct my sweet what to say she almost shouts "Sorry English" in english whilst shoving the ticket in a hole and the barrier opening and lots of shouting by me. This followed with a blazing argument over the fact that my credit card may have been raped without me knowing how much for and this whilst I was trying to follow the sat nav, work out which way round to go round roundabouts and not upset or even crash into any local drivers. How the hell I managed it I'll never know.

Camping Paquier Fane is a lovely site just on the edge of Chagny, Bourgogne which is itself a very pretty and typically French town with a good assortment of shops, bars and restaurants all within 5 minute walk of the site. The site sits between 2 very busy railway lines which I believe run all night and day so may not suit very light sleepers. We didn't think it was too bad at all.

The young couple that run the site are very friendly and pleasant and I will miss my little chats with the husband (I never did find out his name) we would have first thing in the morning when I picked up our ordered baguette and croissants. They have free wifi there which was plenty fast enough to stream You Tube videos etc.

During the week we were there it was very noticeable the drop in temperature in the evenings and nights and I made the decision we needed to get much much further south so I planned our next leg of the journey to end up on the south coast of France, a 6 hour drive by tolls or 12 without, tolls it was then (oh no, more shouting).

We set off Saturday morning with a half made plan that we may stop at an Aire on route to break the journey. Well that's what Ann thought, I was determined to do it in one go.

We had to go along three lots of toll roads and it appears Ann has got it sussed now and we pass without incident or any shouting. It was quite noticeable that it was getting warmer and warmer the further south we drove and the landscape and buildings started to have a very Mediterranean look.

All was going great and we finally turned off along a very narrow road towards Loupian and our site. Just 100 or so meters from the site some woman in a big 4×4 that has clearly no idea of how wide her vehicle is and hanging over our side of the road hits our wing mirror cracking the casing and upsetting Ann. Fortunately the glass in the mirror remained undamaged. I was unable to do anything to avoid this as there was a deep ditch just inches from my wheels on the right. She knew damn well she was in the wrong as whilst I stopped she didn't.

Le Camping Municipal is a large site with large shaded pitches just outside the village Loupian. Each pitch is shaded on three sides by its own trees (watch this though as when I tried to pull in to my pitch I got caught up in the overhanging branches as I cut in too close, much to the amusement of our new neighbours).

There is free wifi here which is the fastest we have had on any site anywhere to date. You need to ask for this at reception and they will give you a little slip of paper with log on details which will give you 6 hours internet per day. If you need more than that, which I do, just tell them you have got other laptops you want to connect and they will give you another one or maybe more. When you do first log on you MUST watch a short advert before you are able to use it but seeing as its free I really didn't mind.

Loupian itself is a typically lovely little village with a few shops, bars and restaurants and is built up around the part ruined Chapel of Saint-Hippolyte dating back to the twelfth century which makes this a fascinating place to explore with narrow passages winding around the buildings.

Broken Bed.

After a couple of enjoyable days at Loupian a storm sweeps across southern France and after 2 days of rain we are left on site which is coated in mud. Everything at ground level is coated in a thin layer mud especially the mats we use in the awning. To be fair it did rain very heavily and I read a few days later that more than 4,000 people across the region spent the night in emergency centres.

Oh yes and I broke the bed. Yep the fat boy trying to climb over the missus in the early hours of the morning to go to the loo finally found the weak spot and it gave way. In a desperate attempt not to do any further damage I let my legs go from underneath me and crashed to the floor, just where one of the dogs usually sleeps. Thank heavens the little madam had managed to sneak up onto the bed and wasn't there otherwise I would have broken her too.

Enough is enough and time to move on earlier than planned. Yes I know neither of those events warrants moving on but hey, any excuse. So we got everything cleaned up, well Ann did anyway and I sat pondering on how best to fix the bed. It was just a case of refitting the broken runner and four screws should do the job and make it stronger as well.

We chose to stay in France for one more week and a bit before we crossed into our new country of residence for this winter and turned out to be quite a good idea.

Les Criques de Porteils is a 5 star site situated between Argeles-sur-Mer and Collioure right on the coast above some cliffs which have three sets of privately accessed steps down to three small coves with shingle beaches.

On arrival, I was shown around by one of the staff, all of which speak english as well as other languages, to choose my pitch. We quickly found the perfect pitch giving us a view over the Mediterranean sea one way and a view of the Alberes mountains the other.

The site is very clean and well run with a shop and restaurant on site as well as a heated swimming pool. There is plenty of fantastic walking in the area with stunning views to enjoy under the Mediterranean sun. For dog owners, this is a dog friendly site and they even supply poo bags free of charge to encourage you to clear up behind your dog.

We liked the site so much we extended our stay an extra week than was originally planned. I have to admit sitting working with a view out over the Mediterranean sea is very difficult to beat.

Mountain Pass.

Thanks to a suggestion by one of my clients, Dave, we decided to cross the border from South West France into North East Spain via the old road rather than the motorway. This turned out to be the most brilliant of decisions and a scenic delight. To get there we needed to drive along three mountain passes with hair pin bends, solid rock walls to one side and sheer drops of hundreds of feet on the other and all on roads just wide enough for us to pass oncoming cars, larger vehicles were another matter but fortunately they were few and luckily only on the slightly wider bits.

All the while the views on this very sunny and hot day were stunning. I wish I had stopped at the few spots there were to stop but I was on a roll and loving the driving challenge. They took us up high before dropping down to a town with a harbour and then back up high again to then drop all the way back to sea level and another town before our final climb up to the old Spanish border post.

It's kind of a shame the border post has been completely abandoned and left to rot as it has the potential of being quite a good tourist spot with the stunning view and buildings which could serve as host to a museum, shop and coffee shop maybe.

As we descended down the mountain, we came across a petrol station where I could fill up but was somewhat crowded with a coach party that had stopped there. Whilst I was waiting in the queue I noticed a couple of gentlemen looking into the windows of our Motorhome. So giving up my place in the queue I went over to see what the hell they thought they were doing.

With a mixture of Spanish, english and some hand signals it turned out they were trying to work out how we managed to fit on the benches in the rear lounge to sleep as they were far too short to fit a fully grown adult. I explained again with our communication mixture that the bit in the middle pulls out and makes a double bed. Handshaking was then done and I went back to join my queue which had just about gone by then.

The site we decided to stop at was Aquarius Camping which is located next to a large sandy beach on the Costa Brava near Girona. It is an exceptionally well run site and very clean. The toilets and showers are the very best we have experienced so far in our travels and puts the UK ones to shame. There is a restaurant, bar, beach bar and large supermarket that sells an extensive array of stuff including some camping equipment etc. All the staff speak several languages including English.

The site is very popular with Germans, so my wife was happy as she is half German and speaks the lingo very well, and it turned out to be half term for many German schools so was very busy. We quickly made good friends with the families who were our immediate neighbours and were invited to join one of the families at their table at the beach bar on Sunday which was having its last day of the season and selling all its drinks for one euro. Needless to say we all got rather drunk whilst talking and listening to the live bands the bar had put on.

There is little else close by and is a somewhat remote location. This is not a big issue at all as with the sandy beach and the onsite facilities and restaurant there is no need to leave the site other than walking the dogs. The beach is quite windy a lot of the time and so is very popular with wind surfers. There are various excursions organised by the camp site for those that want to explore further afield.

Whilst we were at our last site in France, we found out what a Mistral wind is, to our cost. One of the arms of our awning was ripped away from the body of the van without any warning, well thats not quite true, we did get a little notice as the wind had suddenly started and we were just thinking we best get it in incase it gets worse.

Well it did, right then! We had some help from our French neighbours and a very nice Dutch chap that was passing and between our joint multicultural European emergency workforce we got it held up in place and wound back in.

I rang the insurance company and found out that the damage would be covered and there was a £400 excess. Since I would not be returning to the UK anytime soon could I get an estimate and let them know.

Having arrived at Aquarius and settled in I enquired as to if they knew of anyone local that could look at it. Fortunately there was a shop at the top of the road (http://caravan-service.eu) that also had a mobile repair van that could come out to us and have a look for us. We were told by one of the other campers that he was very good and not expensive and they were right. He turned up and repaired the damage in no time at all and only charged us 70 Euros.

Opposites.

Another 5 hours drive southwards and we stopped off for a week at Camping Torre la Sal 2 which is our first stop at a site that is open all year round. It's a very well run site with good size pitches and good facilities. Each pitch has its own outside sink with running cold water which Ann thought was marvellous. I just thought it a little odd, but hey the missus was happy.

It's a very large site split into two by a little used road to another site next door and a back road to a small fishing village one and a half kilometres away. The crossing between the two halves is patrolled by a security guard to keep it safe. One side is right next to a beautiful fine sandy beach. The site also has three swimming pools two restaurants extensive sporting facilities and its own bull ring which only seems to hold events during the summer season.

Just down the road are large apartment complexes which at the time of our visiting were totally deserted. I found it very spooky and weird walking down a long tree lined avenues with buildings all around and totally deserted. I felt like I was in one of those disaster movies where an entire city had been abandoned due to some deadly disease or nuclear accident. Even the sprinklers were still doing their job in the early morning just before dawn because they left in such a hurry and forgot to turn them off. Just before dawn? I hear you say, yes thats right, I am out then as Sasha has quickly worked out that its then, when its nice and cool, she can get a nice long walk before settling down for the day under the van and watching the comings and goings of other residents of a site. She is a very smart dog.

There are three swimming pools to choose from one of which is covered in the winter. The two outside pools are only open out of season if weather permits. One of which has a bar in the middle of it but alas is only open during the summer season. The weather was very nice and they had opened one of them. I was exceptionally pleased to see my first couple of topless ladies and hoped this was going to be a regular visual treat now we have made it far enough south. It turned out this was to be the first and only sighting during our entire stay in Spain.

Having spent the last two sites that were predominantly occupied by our German cousins I thought that maybe, being open all year, this would be one of the sites I have heard so much about where all my fellow countrymen winter. No this one was even more German orientated with a couple Dutch thrown in for good measure.

I found it very frustrating that when I am trying, and I do mean trying, to learn Spanish when everyone around me is talking German and the only bit of real practice I get is saying good morning or whatever to the security guard as I pass him three or four times a day on the way in and out with the dogs.

Whilst it is a great site, it is somewhat out in the middle of nowhere and what was close, was deserted and all closed up. I decided we would move on after only a week but this time, try and find a site in, or at least close by, a town. Oh yes and we need to start looking for somewhere to fill up the LPG as we have now emptied one bottle and on to our second. Its lasted nearly a whole month so very pleased with it.

We had noticed on the way through Spain that none of the motorway service stations have LPG unlike France that all have them, well most anyway, and checking the snooper sat nav it seems this may be a major issue as none were being shown anywhere within a 60 km radius. Doing a Google I found http://www.mylpg.eu/stations/spain and looks like there are plenty of places. (This is a very useful site and worth bookmarking). This just left me to search out where we would head to next.

Deciding to head to the ancient fishing village of Calpe in the heart of the Costa Blanca. Whilst this was only a 3 hour journey, it ended up taking us considerably more time. Not because we made a small detour to fill up with LPG and Diesel but because we got held up when the A7, just outside Valencia, which was closed due to an accident and vehicle fire, but not just any vehicle, it had to be a lorry carrying gas cylinders. What gas I don't know as by the time we got to go past it they were all blackened from the fire. We did get chatting to a lovely Spanish couple next to us who told us this kind of hold up was very unusual and I explained it was a daily occurrence in the UK especially on the M25 London orbital (or outer London car park as its affectionally known). I have to say that being stuck in traffic in the beautiful Spanish sunshine is much preferred to the M25 with the cold and rain lashing your windows.

We finally reached Camping Calpemar which is a small site situated just a few hundred meters from the town and the beach. It has three sizes of pitches available small (suitable for camper vans and small motorhomes although you could squeeze a 7 meter MH in there), the medium size (more suitable for the larger motorhomes) and the big (reserved for those with the big A class's and RV's).

I opted for the medium size pitch which cost a little more (4 Euros a night extra) so we had plenty of space for us and the girls and managed to get the pitch right next to the restaurant/bar and pool, an absolute bonus I thought.

It looks like we have now passed the furthest south the majority of the Germans are willing to travel as there are only a handful here as far as I can tell. Mostly seems to be Brits with a smattering of other nationalities.

Being close to the town I decided it was a good opportunity to find out if I can get my eyes tested as I am long overdue. Imagine my surprise to find a Specsavers just down the road with english speaking staff and optometrist. It appears this is quite a popular area for the British and just about all the shops here in Calpe are English speaking. Oh and guess what I needed new glasses.

I also popped into a vets to enquire about a couple of rumours I had heard along our travels and seems they were true. Firstly the girls chips need to be scanned and registered here in Spain as they do not have access to the UK databases and if lost and found they are unable to identify who the dogs belong to. And secondly they need some protection against mosquitos in this region of Europe.

Having got all this done and it being lunchtime I thought this would be a good time to seek out some of the local cuisine among many of its bars and restaurants. It didn't take long before I found a large sign outside of a restaurant saying "The original Indian Restaurant". This led me quickly to thinking that I have not had a curry since leaving old Blighty and the thoughts of sampling the local dishes was thrown instantly in the bin.

The Punjabi Curry serves what I can only describe as one of the absolute best in curries. Not only do the staff speaks excellent English but they are very helpful and most attentive. They even prepared a special curry for me as I wanted a Chicken Tikka Masala but a little hotter than normal (I was reasoning that a Tikka Madras was just too hot for the thirty odd degree weather). The waiter even came out with a small dish of the sauce they had prepared for me to try to check it was hot enough. I will certainly be returning during our stay in Caple.

The town, beach and promenade is lovely with such a vast array of shops, bars and restaurants and the warm dry climate makes it an absolute pleasure to wander around the shops. I swear, you could eat out every day of the year and not have to visit the same place twice

If you explore up the hill into the old town, you will be treated to a visual feast of a typical Spanish town of narrow streets suddenly opening up into a square with maybe colourful murals on the walls or a beautiful church.

We stayed here for at least a couple of weeks, not only because I had to wait for my new glasses to be made but because I actually like it here and there is plenty to see and do.

I am constantly reminding my good lady to stop worrying about what other people think as with our nomadic lifestyle and the sheer size of Europe the chances of ever seeing anyone around us again is virtually nil. I need to learn learn to shut up and keep my thoughts to myself. We were sitting enjoying an intimate little gathering and the entertainment put on by Camping Calpemar when we are approached by a lady who recognised us from Briarfields.

I would like to say that I am such a memorable chap but alas this is not so. It's our two huskies, Ellie and Sasha, they have recognised. So any chance of hiding from past encounters are just never going to happen. It seems the girls are getting quite famous as we were also approached a few days later by another couple who had again recognised them but not from a previous site but from my blog and Facebook activity.

I suppose that means I am now going to have to start behaving a little better than before but then again I have every intention of growing old very disgracefully and have fun to boot so if you do have the very misfortune of being in the same place as us at the same time sorry nothing personal just having fun and your more than welcome to join me.

Christmas.

Before reaching our final destination for Christmas we spent a week at Camping Las Torres which is located in the valley of a horseshoe of mountains a few kilometres from Puerto de Mazarrón. The web site and information in the ACSI book and app are somewhat inaccurate and out of date. For example, the web site says it's 800 meters from the beach. This is grossly inaccurate as it's more like 2 to 3 kilometres away. The ACSI information says its run by two english ladies. This was out of date as according to one of the permanent residents here they left some years ago. Despite these failings the site is quite pleasant and very quiet and well kept.

The area is dry and very stony land that has not been farmed for several years, although the signs of it once being farmed is still there in ploughed furrows. The fact they have not been flattened out after this period of time tells the story of a lack of any wind or rain here for years. The one thing that really strikes you is just how quiet it is. But it's more than that, it's completely absent of sound at all. Just walk a short way away from the site, stop, hold your breath and you'll see what I mean. Nothing not a single sound, it's very bizarre. Yes there is a road but very little traffic runs along it and if you walk deeper into the valley away from the road even that sound seems to vanish (or maybe just nothing was on the road at the time).

It's a long walk or cycle to anywhere from here and the meagre shop sells a few essentials but not much at all. The restaurant seems to only do Tapas most of the time and is closed on Mondays. So whilst it makes a very pleasant stay do stock up before you arrive unless you have better transport than just a bicycle.

Our stop over Christmas and new year is to be the longest, voluntary, stop since we started traveling 11 months ago and was planned to be six weeks in length. Our only other stop at that period of time was forced upon us when I tore my tendons in Dorset. 11 months have gone by so quickly and looking at the map we have travelled a long way.

We booked into Camping Cabopino for 6 weeks until just after the new year. The site is very nice indeed although the internet is a bit on the slow side, not good, there are plenty of places to eat close by with an Italian and a Indian restaurant on the door step as well as a bar and restaurant on site. We did try the Italian restaurant and whilst expensive, the food was excellent. The onsite restaurant is much better priced and the food is good. The english cooked breakfasts they do are certainly the best though, and very cheap. The beach is close by (300 meters) with a couple of beach bars and several more in the marina which is not far along the beach.

The girls are really pleased with the site as well as they have a small secure compound where they can be let off the lead to have a run around and play.

One morning at 2am and we're both up and fighting the wind for our sun awning and awning room. This was complicated by the Christmas lights and decorations draped and wound around and had to be quickly cut out. Then of course sleep was just a non starter for at least another hour or so not helped by the thought I will still have to be up at sunrise as Sasha one of our Huskies will INSIST she HAS to have her walk. Ellie, the other husky, just doesn't care. Bet you can't guess which ones my favourite today.

So there I am just laying there wide awake, following our victory against the weather, building an excellent case as to why I should purchase a drive away awning. I lasted a full 15 minutes before I get out of bed and switching the laptop on to do some research.

Yep I was right, a drive away awning is exactly what we need. In fact a really good one. One that I can use in extreme weather conditions half way up K2 in winter. Okay so I'm never going to be pitching up there or then but at least I know I can if I want.

I decided on the Vangard Kela and had a ring round a couple of places later in the morning to see who had one and can get it shipped to Spain before Christmas. It's gonna be tight, but we should have it just in time. Fingers crossed.

A week or so before Christmas it dawned on me that I had not done anything about a present for Ann and had not a clue what I was going to. I was pondering what to do whilst walking the dogs one afternoon and decided to walk them down towards the beach. This involved walking over the road bridge that goes over the main road and is guarded on both sides by metal barriers.

Sasha for some reason suddenly decides to go under the barrier into the road and in my attempt to stop her made her panic (she is a real panickier at the slightest thing) and immediately tried backing away and slipped out of her harness just as a van was coming over the bridge. Fortunately the nice man saw what was happening and slowed down allowing me to get her back off the road.

It turns out he was from a company called "Doggy Day Care" that takes your dogs for the day and have a large secure compound with a swimming pool for them. They collect your beloved pooches in the morning and drop them off back to you that evening.

It occurred to me this could be very fortunate and if I could book the encounter with dolphins experience I had been reading about at a Dolphinarium it would be the perfect present for Ann who had always wanted to swim with dolphins.

Booking it online for a week or so before Christmas and calling Doggy Day Care and getting the girls booked in I decided it would be a good idea to hire a car for the day as a Taxi would be very expensive as it was quite long way away.

Having got used to driving in a right hand drive vehicle on the right hand side of the road I thought no problem, it will be easy. I had booked it at the reception of the site were on and told to go there on the day of collection at 10 am.

On the day of collection I went up to reception expecting to collect the car then have a little drive around the site to get used to it before venturing out on to the road. However, this was not the case at all. A chap had come down from Calahonda, a town a few miles down the road where the car hire company was located, to collect me and take me to the office where they can do all the necessary paperwork. I'm thinking all the way there I hope they are going to take me back and not expect me to find my own way.

Guess what? Yep, that's exactly what didn't happen. Having completed the paperwork, gave me a complimentary bottle of wine for Christmas (really!) I was shown a car parked out on the road and given the keys. Oh great, not only do I have to find my own way back without my trusty sat nav but I've got to cope with a left hand drive car. Oh well if Jeremy Clarkson can do it so can I, I hope.

Now I was quite happy driving on the right hand side of the road so this should be OK and despite having to sit on the wrong side of the car the pedals are still the same way round, that was a relief I tell you, but hold on…. they've put the gear stick on the wrong side. How the hell am I supposed to change gear with my right hand? Errr, are the gears in the same place? Phew they are.

So I sit there for several minutes, no doubt to the amusement of the car hire staff, and fiddle around to see if I can do the gear changes with the wrong hand. Mmmmm not so bad think I can get the hang of this.

Fortunately, the road it's parked on is quite quiet so I pull out and head down the road. Bang, ouch, wrong hand to change gear. Get to the roundabout slow down, bang, ouch, wrong hand, sod it. Take what I believe is the correct exit (it was) bang, f****, wong hand AGAIN, and this goes on several more times at least and I hate Jeremy Clarkson now, smug git.

Slowly I start to remember which hand to use and things improve. Anyone who thinks that using pain to teach doesn't work is an idiot. It does, I am now using my right hand to change gear like a pro to prove it and my left hand has some nice bruises by way of a reminder.

By the time I get back to the site I am beginning to get it but I am still very not happy about having so much car on my right hand side and don't believe I will really ever get used to it (its not natural). So when it comes time to upgrade the motorhome think I will stick with a right hand drive even tough I won't be spending very much time at all in the UK.

The trip to Selwo Dolphinarium was a marvellous day out and worth every penny, well cent. It's illegal in Spain to actually swim with dolphins, but they do the next best thing. Donning a pair of waders you enter the water and stand on a platform waist deep in water with a guard rail between you and the dolphins. A trainer then explains an awful lot about dolphins and you get to touch and stroke them. They then teach you some hand signals to get the dolphins to do a few tricks which when you're that close to them is amazing.

My favourite moment is where the trainer gets you to splash your dolphin whose reaction is frighteningly fast and head buts the water, along with a lot more and soaks you. They video all this for you as well as getting you to pose for a photo with your dolphin which you can then buy afterwards if you wish.

Later that day, Doggy Day Care dropped the girls off at the appointed time. Having eaten they then slept for the whole evening and all through the night. They were both clearly very tired happy dogs who have had even more fun than we had. The chap had told us they had a great day playing with two Labradors and were in and out of the pool all day.

Our friend Martin flew over to spend a wonderful Christmas with us although it was extremely bizarre walking around in the warm sun in shorts and t-shirt. It really didn't feel like Christmas and felt odd wishing everyone you pass a Merry Christmas.

Having had a very nice Christmas dinner at the Italian restaurant we took the girls for a walk down to the beach and walked all the way along to the Playa de Nudista which is Spanish for Nudist Beach so our friend can go skinny dipping in the sea on Christmas day. I kid you not, he really wanted to do this, and no, I didn't.

Over the weeks we made many new friends and really love the site so much so that I made the decision we would extend our stay here another 4 weeks which was no problem when enquiring at reception. It came as quite a surprise to me that I would not want to move on having got the wander bug so bad during the year but hey somethings just work out.

Sightseeing.

Boxing day and I was back up at the airport picking my two sons up to spend a few days with us. This was an opportunity to do a bit more sightseeing further afield since I had the car and two boys needing entertaining.

Going to and from the airport I kept traveling under a cable car that went up a mountain so thought that might make a good trip out. It was the Teleferico Benalmadena. We arrived there somewhat early and had to wonder around the town and grab some breakfast and a coffee before returning to the entrance.

We boarded the car and climbed up to the top of the mountain to see some spectacular views. The boys took the path to climb up higher while I sat in the fast food place they have there with a coffee as it was quite cold and windy up there.

Weather permitting they do a birds of prey display but alas not for us as the wind was too strong for the birds to fly. It's while we were being told this that another member of staff came over to tell us they need to evacuate us off the mountain right now as the wind is getting too strong for the cable car to run.

The trip down was a lot more rough than on the way up with the car swinging around quite worryingly. Then it suddenly stops and we just sit there with the car being played with by the wind. I sit there trying to look all calm and collected so not to frighten my two boys but inside I am sh****ng myself. It seemed like ages but eventually we continued our journey to the bottom and alighted all safe and sound.

Seeing that Gibraltar was not very far we decided it would be nice to give that a visit as none of us have been there. I had heard that the queues to get over the border can be very long I decided that we would drive close to the border, park up and walk over.

We found an on street parking place less than 5 minute walk from the boarder, which surprised me. As we walked over the border there seemed to be little interest in passport control on either side.

Once through you immediately have a taxi desk on one side and a tour company on the other and just outside is the border are bus stops. We thought that doing a guided tour to start off would be a good plan so booked a tour that takes in St Michaels caves, the apes and the war tunnels.

The guided tour is done on a 8 seater taxi where the driver also doubles as your tour guide. These guys really know their history and are so full of interesting stories as they drive you around. It is also made very clear that Gibraltarians' are very proud of their history and very, very proud to be British.

Space is very limited on the rock and as such thousands of Spaniards cross the border every morning to work there. These facts makes any action by the Spanish government over the rocks sovereignty very complex and difficult.

You are given just enough time in each location to have a good look round although I would have liked a little more time at the war tunnels. Up on the rock you are told not have anything easily accessible in your pockets as whilst it is illegal to touch or feed the apes, they are well aware of this, so may decide to see what you have of interest to them.

At the end of the tour, our driver dropped us off at the main shopping area where you can find bars and restaurants as well as souvenirs and of course duty free shops to stock up with booze and tobacco. Do be aware there are limits to what you are allowed to take back across to Spain though. We did hear of a story where an English family was stopped at the border and searched. The customs officers were very baffled as to why they had no cigarettes or tobacco on them. Even those who don't smoke take stuff over the border as it's so cheap duty free and easily sold.

Having had a nice fish and chip lunch (well we are in the UK, just had to be done), had a good wander around and purchased the maximum tobacco products allowed. We headed back to the border. It's not a very long walk back and you have to walk across the middle of the Gibraltar airport runway as it divides the border crossing and the rest of Gibraltar. I did point out to the boys that as far as I am aware this is the only airport in the world where pedestrians can walk across the runway so is a pretty unique experience.

We thought there was little interest in passport control in crossing over to Gibraltar, but there are even less going back to Spain. No one at all on either passport controls and the Spanish customs hall you walk through was deserted. I was very tempted to go dump our stuff back in the car and then go back over to get another load of fags from the kiosk close to the border but I was tired and couldn't be bothered.

New Year.

The boys returned home leaving Ann and myself alone once again. The on site bar had organised food and live music to see the New Year in with. So for the first time in many years we went out for the evening to see the New Year in and had a great time with the many new friends we had made on the site over the last 6 weeks.

New years day was once again to serve up a disaster but this time with family back in the UK. We received the bad news that Ann's father has had a stroke and is in hospital. Having spoke to the hospital staff the following day as to its severity it was decided we will travel back to the UK as its very likely he is going to need some help and support so we get everything packed up ready to leave first thing in the morning.

Programming the Sat Nav for Dover via the tunnel it tells me it's over 2,000 km and will take in excess of 30 hours (won't be doing that in one go then). The plan is to drive till about 4pm and then search out a stop over or camp site for the night.

We left a little later than planned with a full tank of water, empty waste tank and loo and head in the opposite direction so we can top up the LPG and might as well top up the diesel as well. We stopped along the way at a Cafe/Bar for Bacon, Egg and Chips (well turned out as fried potatoes but never mind) plus 2 cups of coffee each for a mere 20 Euros, the price of one cup of coffee in a UK motorway service station. I love Spain.

After 5 hours of driving and 248 miles we find a secure parking place at Parador de los Galanes, Mazanares where we paid 5 euros to park for the night among the lorries in a nice secure compound. Having got our heads down nice and early, we were woken at 3am by a rave going on at a stadium just down the road. After an hour or so of not being able to get back to sleep I thought sod it I might as well drive rather than just lie here.

We got up made a cuppa, gave the dogs a walk round the compound and got ready to leave. This is where we found out how secure the compound was. Totally locked up with no way of getting out even through the, locked, side gate. It took me nearly half an hour to attract the garage attendant to open the gates.

After filling up with diesel we set off down the road to hear a loud clanging noise coming from underneath the van near the rear axle. I pulled over and got Ann to jump up and down while I crawled underneath to have a looked but blowed if I could see anything. Off I drive again with this banging, but the handling is no different so don't think it's a problem with anything important. After a couple of hours, tiredness started to get hold of me so pulled off into a service area and we got our heads down for a couple of hours.

Nicely refreshed we did make good progress and were soon not too far from the French border. With tiredness catching up with me again in the latter part of the afternoon so searched for somewhere to stop and found a camp site 45 minutes in the right direction.

Having had a good nights sleep we made excellent progress on day 3, crossing the Spanish/French border and traveling up as far as Saintes where we parked up in a free municipal aire.

Just before we crossed the border we had to travel over and through some wonderful mountains and scenery with some dramatic changes in weather. At one point, we were in very thick fog and entered a long tunnel through a mountain to appear out the other side in brilliant sunshine and clear skies.

Our main purpose for trying for an aire in a town was to see if we could find a vets so I can get the dogs checked and wormed as per DEFRA's requirement. As it goes luck would have it there was a vets just down the road and were seen and all sorted straight away for 40 euros each. So they were good to enter the UK.

There are a couple of other motorhomes on this aire with us and one looks like he has been here a while and works locally so I guess it's a safe place. Either way we were not bothered as the girls will stay on guard all night.

We have made it to Calais after an exceptionally long drive and a lot of money on tolls. So after a total of 27 and a half hours of actual driving (4 days in reality) and a distance of 1340 miles we have traveled from the bottom of sunny Spain to the cold and miserable tip of northern France. I hadn't appreciated just how far we had actually traveled down to Spain since we had done it over a number of weeks, but the continuous drive back north ably shoved it in my face.

We spent the night in the Carrefour carpark in Calais and then go find the Eurotunnel in the morning. I thought this was probably best rather than crossing tonight as I am dubious about driving on the wrong side of the road again in the dark. On top of that I was bloody knackered.

We turned up to the Eurotunnel nice and early and went straight to the pet centre where the dogs and their documentation were checked all OK. Since we had not pre-booked they were able to do this for us and oh what a mistake it was not to book in advance. €336.00 for the one way trip. Next time I must make sure were booked in advance.

The trip went smoothly, well except for the fact I broke the bed, again!, and poor Ellie was clearly very confused that the van was moving but I wasn't in the driver's seat. She kept looking at the empty seat and then me with a very worried look on her face.

We drove straight to Southampton, well via a B&Q to get some screws to fix the bed, and booked into Sunnydale Farm Camping and Caravan site and were surprised to find that they only had one pitch available (didn't see that coming). It was quite a nice site although a bit expensive (£130 for 5 nights) but the facilities are good and clean with underfloor heating.

Once we got set up Ann went off to visit her dad who was very pleased to see her. His stroke was a bad one and has left him paralysed down the left side. The doctors said he may make some recovery over the next 18 months with physiotherapy.

We put the new awning up and that night it took a massive battering from the wind and rain. I have to say we are very pleased with it as it coped very well indeed staying up perfectly and staying dry inside. Even the tunnel didn't get much water in it despite it not being sealed down the sides and bottom.

We were already missing Spain dreadfully and I had forgotten what a nightmare it was to walk the dogs in wet muddy fields rather than on sand.

After a few days Eric was transferred up to his home town in Gloucester and we packed up and moved to Briarfields Touring Park booking in for an indefinite period of time.

Alas a few weeks later Eric passed away having caught pneumonia.

R.I.P Eric Morey (1935 - 2015)

Not Again.

Since arriving back in the UK at the beginning of January, we had been pitched up at our favourite site Briarfields.

I got a friend of my stepson, James, to have a look under the van to see if he could see what was causing the clanging on the back end we had developed when travelling up from Spain. He never did identify the exact cause, but he did say that the rear end is sitting on the bump stops and the leaf suspension is not looking very good. The solution would be to add an extra bit to them to support them.

This raised the whole question of weight and if we are travelling overweight. This is one thing that has bothered me for a long time now but not brave enough to visit a weigh bridge to find out for sure. But then again we have twice now reduced everything down to a minimum and my favourite saying to Ann every time she talks about purchasing anything is "NO". So was now wondering if the suspension had always been bad.

I am not sure how we got onto it but at some point we started to think about trading in our motorhome and upgrading to an RV. I guess the seed was originally sown several months back when staying at Southsea where Ann got chatting to a lady that was in one of those big American RVs and was invited in.

Ann has a habit of disappearing for quite a while from time to time as she gets caught up in conversation with someone on her way to or from the washroom or somewhere like that. Not sure why but I went searching for on this particular occasion and, on my way past this ladies RV I hear Ann calling me over saying "You really must come and have a look".

I am given the official guided tour and have to admit it was very nice indeed with such a lot more space than we have with two or three sofas, captains chairs that swivel a full-size fixed bed, wardrobes, toilet, shower, full size fridge freezer. Pretty much everything you have in a house, and more luxurious than our old house as well. Having had a nice chat, we went back to our motorhome and I thought nothing more of it again. After all something like that is well out of my price range.

So here we are again just like when we first thought about a camper van it took on a whole life of its own and started to guide or steer me in very specific directions. Well, I say that. It felt like more fate was once again forcing me down a route whether I wanted to or not. I did resist a little less than last time as fate was very right last time and knows what I want more than I do.

Having done a little research, I worked out we could actually afford an RV and its running costs, providing it runs on LPG and discovered there are quite a few RV dealers about the UK.

Before all this silly talk of RVs had started I had obtained tickets to the motorhome show at the NEC. James took me to this to save Ann having to pack everything up and we dragged along our two youngest sons. After a couple of hours, we had seen all we wanted to, which for me was not much, as no longer saw the point of being there if we were considering changing the van. It was still a consideration in my mind at this point and definitely not a done deal.

Since we had only spent half the day there James thought it would be a great idea to visit an RV dealer on the way back to just have a look. What harm can it do? And we had time to spare.

A quick search on the interweb found us heading to Dreams RV in Bicester which was vaguely (vaguely as in SE instead of SW) on the way back but looked promising with at least one RV listed in my price range.

The staff there were fantastic and very helpful and we only looked a two RVs'. We didn't really need to look at the second as the first one was just perfect and we both felt that Ann would fall in love with it if she saw it. Whilst it was petrol they could do the LPG conversion and it would still be in my price range.

I returned Saturday morning, as arranged with them, with Ann to have a look and see what they would give in part exchange for my motorhome. James and myself were right Ann fell in love with it and after having a look round our motorhome and asking a lot of questions Becky, the very nice lady there, went off to make some calls to get me a price while we continue to crawl all over it opening every cupboard and locker and examining every inch, and it had an awful lot of them.

I had two figures in mind, one that I would like to get for it and not make too much of a loss on it and the other which was the absolute minimum I needed to afford the RV but I would lose a serious amount of money. Well you can imagine my turmoil when I get offered the absolute minimum amount, it meant I could afford to get this RV, the one Ann (and me I suppose) have fallen in love with but means a hefty loss over the 18 months we have had our motorhome.

My dear wife then pipes up she will pay for the LPG conversion if that helps. Oh dear, she really does want it. So deposit gets paid and we sort out a delivery date for around the 15th of the following month but Becky will ring to confirm when she has spoken to the workshop.

For crying out loud, it's happened again only much faster and I have had even less time to fight the inevitable and less time to do much research (I love my research). Just two things, though. 1. It's left-hand drive (I wasn't comfortable with a little, left-hand drive last year in Spain and 2. It's big. No it's massive. Our van is 7 meters in length, but this thing is another 4 meters longer and looks nearly twice as wide. Oh yeah and sitting in the driver's seat you are a long way from the road even on the left its long way to the side of the vehicle.

We now had to wait a few weeks to take delivery. This was mainly because we had previously organised to visit our friend Kath up in Lincoln and stay on her drive for a week. This had to be done in our old motorhome as her drive way wouldn't be big enough for the RV. This also gave them time to get the LPG conversion done and anything else that needed doing.

Despite having a lovely week with Kath, I really couldn't settle very well as I was in an emotional torment between being excited about getting the RV and scared witless about driving something that was, in all honestly, absolutely massive. As luck would have it Kath's son James is an HGV driver and gave me some great advice which helped to calm my fears, a little.

Everything in our motorhome for the last 18 months that had been just perfect up until now was now irritating me. There was no room, everything was cramped, making up the bed every night and breaking it down every morning was a flipping pain. Funny how things that were okay, were now not, just because we had a bigger solution just on the horizon. This also added to my torment, what if the sale fell through at the last moment and we didn't get it? Oh for heavens sake I hate big changes. I also love big changes as they are so exciting.

Delivery Day.

The big day finally arrived and we arrived at the dealers to find our RV all ready for us to inspect and to be shown how everything worked. Oh my, it was even bigger than I remember it but no time for nerves as there was so much to remember and lots of questions to ask.

Having had a good look round and been through the orientation, turning everything on and off, pressing every button, twiddling every knob and discovering storage space we didn't know was there, we went into the office to complete the paperwork and pay the outstanding balance. Once done, the transfer of all our precious possessions began.

I have sat and pondered on this for some time since but I still cannot fathom how and where the hell all that stuff was stored in that little motorhome. I mean it was vast quantities and took much longer than I expected despite the fact that Ann had done quite a bit of preparation beforehand and we didn't even put stuff away properly, just shoving stuff in any cupboard and piling it on the bed.

The girls were good as gold as all this happened. They just sat in the old van belted into their seats and just watched it all happen. Once everything was moved across we moved the girls over who chose a sofa each, jumped up and looked rather pleased with their new luxurious comfortable seats. They seemed to just simply understand that they have now moved home and were quite happy with it.

After one final look around the old one, to make sure we haven't missed anything, we said our goodbyes and it was time to drive out and onto the road.

Within moments of getting onto the road the screaming started. Being a left hand drive Ann was situated in the "Suicide" seat and since I had to work out just where on the carriageway I had to sit not to be hanging over the middle line she spent some time facing the terrified traffic coming the other way. I did manage to stop poor Ann from being quite so loud, and distracting, but only with a very harsh and very loud "shut the f*** up" (sorry darling).

First of all we needed to get this thing filled up with fuel so following the directions we were given we found the petrol station a few miles down the road where they also sold LPG and despite it being a tight turn onto the forecourt I managed it quite easily and without hitting anything.

The filler for the engine and the domestic LPG are on opposite sides of the RV (why they did this I have no idea as its a flipping pain) so having filled up the engine LPG we drove out and up the road to a roundabout, went right around it and back to the garage so I could pull up on the other side of the pump to fill the domestic LPG and the petrol tank which is on the same side. My goodness, it took a lot of petrol, 100 litres, a nice big tank I thought so should be good if we can't find any LPG when abroad.

I climb back in and off we go towards the site at Cheltenham where we will be staying for a few days before the motorhome show and rally at Newark. It's as I am about to pull off that I notice the petrol gauge is only showing half a tank. Then I thought, hold on, the petrol pump just stopped it didn't do that click thing it does when you're full. Ah, 100 litres is the maximum you can buy at a pump, but that is less than half a tank, oh wow it is a very big tank.

The roads from Bicester to Cheltenham are mostly single carriageway with a few bits of dual carriageway so I had to work out very quickly how close I could get to the side of the road so not to be over the centre line. Being on or just a fraction over is not that much of an issue unless there is an HGV coming the other way doing exactly the same, and they all do, and they don't slow down. The screaming starts up again and I am desperately trying to move over more but without hitting the curb or going in the ditch which is already so close you couldn't get a bean pole between us, well so it seemed at first.

After a few dozen miles of this I started to settle into it and was able to get even closer to the edge without hitting it and Ann started to settle down and let me know quite calmly when I was drifting over the line, although I did notice she was gripping the side of her seat with white knuckles. Whilst sitting at some red traffic lights I glanced behind me at Ellie, one of our dogs, who would normally be fast asleep when we travel, to be lying there wide awake with her paw up on the armrest and claws curled in holding on for dear life. Oh, great that's all I need, thank heavens I can't see the other dog, that would send me over the edge if all three of them were holding on in fear of their lives.

Due to a little confusion over a left turn I was supposed to take we ended up having to go through the centre of Cheltenham at just the wrong time of day as the school run was in full swing and the roads were busy. It went very well and I simply just owned the road and found it a little amusing at the petrified faces of other road users as I bullied my way through. To be fair they simply stayed well clear of me and gave me plenty of room, even the bus drivers were nice to me.

We arrived at our destination quite safely and only once just clipping a curb on a central island which ironically was just a 100 meters or so from the site entrance. Once parked up on our pitch we quickly got set up and began getting organised.

We settled in very nicely and loved everything about it. Everything was perfect and I especially loved the shower and being able to do all my morning ablutions without having to walk down to the shower block in the cold. The day before we had to leave for Newark the heating stops working. After some extensive investigation, I work out it's the control board that has developed a fault.

James came to our rescue again by giving us a small fan heater which turned out to be ideal. I rang the dealers and arranged to pop in there on the way to Newark for them to replace the board for us.

Newark Motorhome show.

Having spent a few days getting organised (well Ann did most of it), we were ready for the next trip. To the Newark motorhome show. This was mostly motorway and allowed me to relax and play with carriageway positioning without worrying about hitting a curb and work out where on the windscreen the edge of the road would be (much further over than I thought LOL).

My plan was to stop twice to fill up the LPG tanks one for one side and the second for the other and also top up the petrol as we will be running the onboard generator for power as we won't be on electric hook up over the weekend. This plan went well and another 100 litres of petrol went in and still was not full, but near enough.

Our first stop was at the dealers in Bicester, which was quite a way out of our way, but hey. It's here I noticed that I had not retracted the TV aerial and was sitting at a very odd angle. Glad we were at the dealers I thought. I tried to wind it down and it went down just fine so I guess no harm done. Phew.

The final approach to the Newark show ground was down a narrow lane (well narrow for us) with no centre white line and I drove down the middle of this until an oncoming car came at which I pulled right over as far as possible and stopped to allow them to squeeze past.

We had a great weekend (although my credit card disagrees and is seriously dented now) and made some great new friends. We did have a little trouble from the generator which had clearly not been run for a long time. Whilst it started okay it proceeded to spit out a lot of muck which gave us some concern. Someone did come over to have a look at it for us the following day where it proceeded to run very sweetly and cleanly so seems it was just the fact it hadn't been run for a long while.

When we came to leave I decided that since there was a very conveniently located RV waste dump on our way out we would have a go at discharging our waste for the first time having a weeks worth of waste in it, even though the lights showing how full the black tank was still showed two-thirds full, but it did that almost immediately so I wasn't very confident it was correct.

It was either going to go well or if anything went wrong was going to be a very unpleasant experience and quite a good spectator sport to boot, at my expense. I could only imagine the scene, me standing there covered in raw sewage with people all around throwing up and laughing at the same time.

I was very careful to make sure the big hose was correctly hooked up and all looked correct. Putting the end of the hose down the hole and making sure I had a good hold of it (didn't want this thing turning on me and giving me a good spraying) I told Ann to pull the handle on the left (I was pretty certain that was the black side). It emptied its contents down the hole surprisingly quickly so called to Ann to close that and open the other which again pushed the grey tank contents out and flushing any residual stuff left in the pipe. So all went well, phew you have no idea of how relieved I was.

The drive back to Cheltenham went even better as I have really got the hang of driving it now and quite honestly love it. Putting my previous plan of topping up the LPG at different services was put into practice but went somewhat badly as it seems not all service stations on the motorways sell LPG (I thought they did but seems not) so having filled up the domestic I carried on to discover we couldn't find another for the engine and ended up running out of LPG before I could fill up again. With a little worry in my heart, I pressed the little button to switch it back to petrol which it did without missing a single beat.

We made it back to Cheltenham just fine and parked up and got settled in for the easter break where we had both my sons visiting and our good friend Martin.

It's only now we discover that there is a problem with the TV aerial and I must have done some damage in leaving it up as we race along the motorway at a heady 50 mph.

On the basis, I do not like heights, well actually I don't mind heights at all. I have done a lot of abseiling in the past and sliding down a cliff or other vertical wall whilst harnessed and roped up doesn't even phase me a little. However, if I am not harnessed and roped up and in control I am not happy even going up as far as the third rung on a ladder. It's not that I am afraid of falling, it's the hitting the ground at a faster speed than I am comfortable with that scares me.

So I ask David, who looks works at Briarfields as the groundsman, and he agrees to pop up and have a look at it for me. It appears I had damaged the coaxial cable by it tilting more than it's designed for and he renders a repair for me.

The girls are much happier with the new living arrangements and clearly love having the extra space not only to be able to stretch out but also to play in.

It looks like Sasha, the escapologist, has settled down much better than we had ever hoped. One afternoon, having chained them up outside a while previously, I went to get them in to find Sasha had wrapped the chain around a post and not having any room to move had backed out of her harness and was just laying by the side of. She hadn't run or even wandered, off. Something very unusual for a Husky. We gave her lots and lots of fuss and a few tasty treats for being such a good girl.

National Motorhome Show.

We spent a weekend at the Peterborough show ground for the National Motorhome Show. It's an impressive show with hundreds of exhibitors selling you everything from American RVs to tap connectors and lots of stuff you never even knew existed let alone needed.

You have a couple of options to visit the show. You can enter as a day visitor or you can stay onsite as a camper. Whilst it's quite possible to get around the show in a day you do miss out on so much more. They provide entertainment in several venues every evening most of which are free and with a very good lineup of artists. On Saturday night, there is the option of paying extra for the main entertainment in the arena which this year was the famous comedian and television personality, Jim Davidson.

You can camp in the public camping area or if you are a member of a group that has organised an area you can book to go with them. Two groups we are members of Motorhome Fun and RV Owners Club both had organised areas. We went with Motorhome Fun for the simple reason we had booked them before joining the RV Owners Club.

When you spend a lot of time on secure campsites as we do as full timers you tend to get used to a relatively safe environment where it's pretty unlikely someone will try to nick your stuff. I am sure it does happen from time to time, but our experience so far is that this is rare. However at these very big events and especially where the general public is let in and have free reign to wander around you need to be a little more security conscious.

Because we have two dogs we tend to not worry too much about undesirables as they will warn us if something is wrong or should deal with it for us if required. You would think so, wouldn't you? Well seems we were wrong. They are flipping useless.

Ann had gone off with our friends Dave and Doreen to look around the show leaving me with the dogs. Having had a hard morning looking round the show and denting my credit card, I decided to have a bit of a well-earned afternoon kip.

I was woken by a female eastern European accent that was very close by. Either just outside the window or inside the RV. I thought that Ann had returned and brought someone with her. As I got up, I heard the door slam shut and could see the dogs just laying there clearly not having moved. Looking out the window all I could see was a blond haired lady walking away.

Seeing as the dogs hadn't moved and only having just woken up, I began to doubt what I thought I had heard and maybe was the tail end of a dream or me just going senile. A few minutes later the wind caught the door and opened it as it was not shut properly and seeing as I know I had shut it properly was confirmation that it wasn't a dream at all and some stranger had opened our door. Flaming useless dogs could not even be bothered to get up and warn them off. There SACKED and I told them so.

This woman didn't completely disappear as she appeared a couple of times more on the main roadway near our spot and the second time I snapped a couple of pictures of her on the mobile. I called security and recounted the story who was very interested in seeing the photo and asked me to hang on to it in case they needed to get the police involved.

I never did hear any more about this and I wonder if it was a perfectly innocent mistake by someone looking for someone but does make you think. And I am still angry with my useless mutts.

While we were there we had a call from the new owner of our old motorhome. The chap rang to ask if we had left the electric hook up cable with it, as thought that maybe the dealers had taken it out to sell separately. I told him we hadn't and after a further discussion it appears they hadn't done any sort of hand over with him at all as he didn't know what some of the switches did. He was also very surprised to be told he had 2 leisure batteries and had no idea there was a solar panel on the roof. I also took the opportunity to warn him about the tank heaters and not to leave them in overnight if he is not on EHU.

Overall we had a great weekend made new friends and caught up with old ones, chatted and received lots of helpful hints and advice. Well worth going.

Enhancements & Planning.

While we were based in one place for a while I took the opportunity to make a few changes to the RV.

I replaced the old stereo from one with a tape deck, I mean come on we got rid of all our cassette tapes years ago and even CD's are a thing of the past, to a media player one that I can connect my iPhone to. It wasn't a terribly simple thing to do and had to cut the old connector wires and the new ones and join the two halves to make a new one. Luckily the colours in each connector wire all matched with each other.

Two things I have noticed when driving our RV. 1. It has some pretty big blind spots close to the sides and 2. It's quite hard to judge just how close you are to the side of the road or the centre. I think I have got it sussed on the left side, but the right I rely on my co-pilot, Ann, to tell me. This is okay, but she doesn't drive (well except me up the wall) and she only tells me once I am over it. Not something useful like you are 6.6343773mm from the white line.

This, in all reality, does not matter too much, most of the time, here in the UK where I am driving on the wrong side of the road (remember it's a left-hand drive). But once in lands of a foreign nature its no longer going to be a white line I slip over a bit but a kerb or a concrete block or a 600 meter drop. The solution to both these issues is a couple of kerb (or look down) mirrors. So now I can see for myself how close I am with the added bonus that I can see any sneaky cyclists having a rest on the side of me.

Last year we planned up as far as the tunnel and after that we just made it up as we went along and hoped we could get into any sites etc. It went very well and was not turned away once. But that was with our Compass Rambler motorhome. Now we have an 11 meter RV there will be quite a few sites that just won't be able to take our size or have facilities to dump our waste so best thought it was probably better to research and book.

Using several resources, mostly ACSI, I identified several sites and sent emails asking if they could take our length and have the facility to handle our waste. I got some lovely replies and only two required a deposit.

The journey will take us a total of 2,398 miles over the course of nearly 4 months where, at our final stop, we have booked in for 3 months which will take us to March next year where I suppose I will need to plan the trip back to our starting point for July when the MOT will be due again.

A rough calculation makes that a total cost of fuel at just over £1,000 which spread over 4 months will be £250 each month, but we will see.

Alas, we can't stay at Cabopino, where we wintered last year. We would have liked to as we made some great friends there and are there every year. Whilst they can take the size but do not have facilities to dump our waste. Such a shame.

So all in all I am pretty happy. I have everything all planned and booked from now until March next year including a few rallies with the Funsters between now and end of July when we start.

Bang.

We were heading up the M5 on our way to Thetford, Norfolk for a Motorhome Fun Rally when less than an hour into our 4 hour journey the is a very loud BANG which sounded very much like something compressed had exploded.

I immediately pulled into the hard shoulder and realised I was rapidly running out of hard shoulder as we were approaching an exit as well. This left me with little choice but to break harder than I was happy about but did manage to stop still in the hard shoulder.

I looked round the RV and could see nothing wrong at all so guessed it was not us but maybe the lorry that was passing us at the time. Being so close to the junction meant getting straight back onto the M5 was not really a sensible option so I pulled out onto the exit ramp and rejoined it on the other side.

All was well until we were about 30 minutes from our destination and BANG again. This time, there was no hard shoulder to abort onto as we were on a dual carriageway. I realised that I felt nothing of this in the steering or the vehicle at all. Very strange indeed and totally baffling. If it was a tyre, which is what it sounded like, what are the odds of 2 going in one trip and anyway when I looked last time I couldn't see anything wrong.

We reached the rally and got parked up and put the levelling jacks down. Ann then says that the rear wheel doesn't look right, it looks like it's on a lean. I had a look it appeared the outer back tyre was blown and not sitting straight in the rim. Ah so it was a tyre blow out we had, what about the second, or first, bang? Round the other side, the outer wheel was fine but reaching to the inner one that was in an even worse state than the other side.

It gets even better next as I discover that apparently in rural Norfolk they don't have much in the way in mobile signals and can barely get a signal on one of the phones and none at all on any of the others.

So with a dodgy phone signal I call the breakdown service and explain the situation and I am in no hurry to get this sorted, I repeated this a few times in our conversation but seems they are unable to comprehend such a phrase so just ignored it. I was told that someone will be with me in the next 90 minutes.

About an hour later someone from their commercial department called me to say that because it was two tyres and on an HGV they would have to tow me, where do I want to go? Ah, this could be a problem as I need to find someone who has these in stock. I told them this and said I will call them back.

I rang an RV specialists I know in Cheltenham and speak to them who tell me they have 4 in stock but can't fit them but can ship them out to me. I explain this is not a great deal of help and after some further discussion they say I can have it towed to them and they will get a tyre company out to fit them for me tomorrow.

I rang back the breakdown company and they take the details of where I want to go and tell me someone will be with me within 90 minutes. About an hour later, yes you guessed it, they rang me back to say they were having trouble finding a low loader that is available and will keep me updated.

While we are waiting our friend Martin turns up and says he is happy to take Ann and the 2 dogs in his car there leaving me to go with the RV.

An hour or so later I have still heard nothing and I am getting very fed up not knowing what's happening and today is also my 3rd day of giving up smoking and I am so very close to cracking. I call them again and whilst waiting to be put through to the commercial department they ring me. They still are unable to get the low loader and apologise for not calling me back sooner. The chap on the phone, a different one to whom I was speaking before, then wants to confirm with me it is two tyres and would it be all right, if they have them, to replace them here? Yes please, that's what I wanted in the first place rather than have to end our weekend just as it started. The only trouble is they may not have them because of the odd size. He takes the details and says he will call back.

Ten minutes later he is back on the phone to say yes they are pretty sure they have them and will call back in 10 minutes if not but otherwise will be with me in 90. It must have only been 15 minutes later when a tyre centre pickup truck turns up and out jumps a long, curly haired, small chap named Peter with what sounded like a strong west country accent but could have been a local accent I suppose.

Having been shown which tyres need doing he then starts to try and work out how to get the shiny wheel trims off. Turns out that out of all the nuts on it only 2 are real and that's what holds the trim on. The next bit surprised me as having got the wheel off he proceeded to get the old tyre off and the new one on, the hard way. No automatic tyre machine but massive tyre levers and a lump hammer. This chap may have been small but he was strong and very fit as he didn't seem to break into heavy breathing let alone a sweat.

When he comes to do the second tyre, it's now dark and I decide to get my hands dirty and help by holding a torch for him. He took the time to show me a couple of useful points that I can impart on any future tyre fitter that will help them.

By the time it's all done and paperwork signed it's gone 10:30 pm and we both said we wished these call centres would pass on important information like the customer is in no rush and can be done anytime over the weekend. At least then he could have done it in the daylight which would have been much easier.

The rest of the weekend went quite well. Tim and Pippa, good friends we met in Cabopino, lived close by and so came over for a visit on Saturday and we had a most enjoyable time updating each other with stuff in our lives and remembering the good times we had in Spain last year.

The organisers of the rally put on a few events over the weekend of which I think the best was a very competitive moped racing event with, apparently, very few, if any, rules. Whilst I didn't take part myself it was great fun watching.

Well, I say the rest of the weekend went well, that was until we travelled back to Briarfields in Cheltenham. I was very concerned that the other 4 tyres were old and tired (pun intended) and so was on tenterhooks just waiting for a front wheel blow out. When we pulled in to Hopwood services on the M62 with most of our journey competed to fill up with fuel Ann said she could hear a flapping sound.

Stopping by the pump, I got out to find that one of the new tires was completely flat. So I filled up and drove it over to the HGV parking area to ring the breakdown service again. Having explained the story and said I was happy for a tire company to sort it here they organised just that and a chap arrived about an hour later. On close inspection of the ailing tyre it appears that it may have been that the valve extender was not tightened by the other fitter but he changed that valve anyway just in case and left the extender off as I am going to replace them in the next couple of days and we continued without further incident to our destination.

The following day I called Motorhome Medics and arranged to purchase the 4 tires he had in stock along with a valve extension kit and tire covers the entire lot costing just a little under £1,500 OUCH!

I organised ATS to come out and fit them the following day and they arrived nice and early in the morning. Having tried to jack the RV up to find the jack was sinking so had to move off the pitch onto the roadway. As I started to pull out, I heard a STOP being shouted by Ann. Before I could see her in the mirrors it dawned on me we were still connected to the electric, whoops, disaster averted.

It took them ages and £215 to do the four tires and take the old ones away. During which time we were all stuck outside being very bored indeed. Thank heavens it was dry and sunny otherwise it would have been quite unpleasant.

Fun

Time soon came around for two rallies back to back but with the Motorhome Fun crowd. We headed down to Bagwell Farm in Dorset for the first rally.

On the way I had planned on stopping on the first Motorway Services on the M5, John Stayte Services, to top up with LPG. However this was not to happen due to the layout of the services we had no option but to go through to the HGV parking area from where only the HGV side of the petrol station was accessible and the LPG pump was over the other side. From there on we tried in a few other service stations and kept a close eye on every forecourt we passed but there was no more selling LPG on our route.

About 20 miles from Bagwell Farm we ran out of LPG and had to switch back over to that expensive petrol stuff to complete our journey.

I find I am really getting the hang of and very confident with driving on single carriageway roads now and have found I am the exact width of the narrower ones, well except the wing mirrors that hang over both sides. Not really a problem until you get a lorry coming the other way and Ann starts screaming.

Bagwell Farm is RV friendly in as much as they have a place to be able to dump your black and grey waste on the main site and also on the rally field where we were located for the week.

There is plenty of walking around the farm that includes a moderately easy walk down to the water side which will take about 45 minutes to an hour to get there. I am told there is not a beach as such but didn't make it that far whilst there to check it out for myself. The bus stop is 5 minutes walk away with a regular bus service running between Exeter and Poole. Weymouth is your nearest seaside town and will cost you £3 return to get there.

Weymouth is your typical Georgian seaside resort built up around a harbour and port and has a fine white sand beach all of which make it very popular. For those days not suitable for just lazing around on the beach, and let's face it, this is England, not to worry as there are plenty of things to do to suit all tastes in and around Weymouth.

During our visit Weymouth was the host to the D-Day Landings re-enactment and luckily for us, some of them were camping in the rally field next to us giving us an excellent chance to look around some of the WWII restored vehicles and chat to the owners and restorers.

The organisers of our rally did an excellent job of organising several activities during the week including a Hog Roast and several other social get-togethers. It was at one of these gatherings that in my absence (I was in the RV with the dogs) my wife volunteers me to do the Full Monty with a few of the other guys at the next rally to help raise money for the Cancer Research Charity. If you have not seen or heard of the Full Monty it's a film about Six unemployed steel workers form a male striptease act to raise money in which the women cheer them on to go for the Full Monty which means total nudity.

I am well up for this but over the next couple of days the organisers are getting worried and now no longer want complete nudity as it may upset someone and complain to the forum boss. So Ann has the idea and offers to crochet pouches to hide our bits in. This is readily accepted as a good solution. Personally I think its a shame we have to keep the minority happy after all this is for a good charity and if they don't want to see six old blokes willies they can leave before we start.

It soon came round for us all to depart and most of those on the rally were also heading to the next one at Norden Farm. Because we had run out of LPG for the engine we made a small detour to a garage in Dorchester before heading over to rally number 2 ourselves.

The girls love Norden Farm as there is so much for them to smell and watch. It appears they hadn't forgotten their incident with the goat last year and still bear a grudge for getting head butted by one as they stuck their heads through the fence to have a closer look and say hello.

It also appears I have found the one thing they are scared of, cows. Passing the cattle shed every morning they would go to have a closer look and one of the cows would move ever so slightly to have a look at them and the two girls would shoot backwards almost falling over their back legs to get away. This would have me rolling with laughter and I never got tired of it.

Jez and Lyn organised a tremendous amount of activities and social gatherings starting with a cheese and wine tasting on the first evening and finished the week off on Saturday night with a hog roast, a live appearance from Matt Black who's set was absolutely hilarious and entertaining and finally the "Full Fun Monty". The week was packed with the usual array of bike rides and walks visiting various places in the area along with evening get togethers and quizzes.

On Friday, our friend Martin came down from Sussex to stay with us for the weekend and I had a fantastic time out with him on both Saturday and Sunday.

Not only was it Armed Forces day but The Tank Museum in Bovington was holding its annual Tankfest event of which I was lucky enough to get a couple of the last remaining tickets for Sunday the week before, Saturday was sold out.

So Saturday we took advantage of the Swanage Steam Railway that was running an all steam timetable to take us to Swanage. It is your typical Victorian seaside resort town and proudly boasts a Blue Flag sandy beach.

Because it was Armed Forces day the railway station had a few extra displays and events on with a WWII theme. Our favourite was the two young ladies dressed in blue uniforms singing songs popular during the war.

After an enjoyable couple of hours in Swanage we headed back up the line enjoying a locally brewed beer on the train before stopping off at Corfe Castle for a Cream Tea and to look round the very charming village of Corfe and its model village which showed how the castle will have looked before partially demolished in 1646 by the Parliamentarians during the English Civil War. On closer inspection the model did have a model of the model village much to our amusement.

We stayed on at Norden for an extra week after the rally as we were booked in to have some electrical work to be done the following Monday at Vanbitz in Taunton. We stayed for one complimentary night at their camp site Cornish Farm Touring Park so we will be ready at 8:30am the following morning.

The camp site is on the same land as Vanbitz which meant we only had to drive a few yards into their garage first thing. We had fitted a 2KW inverter, 2 x 135ah batteries and a battery management module, this took just about all day. The first half of the day we all sat outside reception on a cloudy and not very warm day and retreated inside to their waiting area for the second half of the day as it started to rain on and off throughout the afternoon.

Having had our RV handed back to us with all the work done we headed back to Briarfields Motel and Touring Park. Heading through Taunton our sat nav took us up a road which we were to discover had been closed at the other end forcing us to have to reverse all the way back up it as it was not wide enough to actually turn round and then out onto a busy main road. Many many thanks to the nice HGV driver that stopped to let us out and help us to piss off a lot of people trying to get home as fast as they can after a hard days work.

We are now comfortably in the position of not being reliant on electric hook up and can still have the 240volt power needed to charge laptops and phones and watch the TV. Depending on how much sun we are blessed with also means we can use it to boil a kettle etc and thats where the battery monitor comes in telling us how far we can push it with power consumption.

This ultimately means we are no longer reliant on campsites and can go wild for as long as we want and make use of aires for waste and fresh water when required. A few experiments and calculations have shown that if we are very careful with water we should be able to go as long a two to three weeks without having to empty and fill up.

Back at Briarfields we stayed off the EHU to give the inverter a good test and despite there be little to no sun and using the electric kettle as well as the array of chargers for phones, tablets and laptops it took a couple of days to drain the batteries down to 50%. I have no doubt that when we reach sunnier climates we will be able to go on for ever.

Back on EHU and all was going well for about a week when Ann decided to put the kettle on but forgot our little electric fan heater was on. This caused the electrics to trip as you would expect. Well you would have thought. No they hadn't tripped but there was no power to any of the sockets except one.

I spent the next two days searching for where the fault could be. I eliminated the new inverter by discontenting it, although did note that there was 240 volts being passed to it via the EHU. The batteries were charging as normal and the one socket over the dining table still worked. This was a real puzzle and very odd. Eventually by chance, when Ann tried to plug the kettle into the working one, I realised that this socket was receiving 110 volts and not 240 as I had assumed.

Monday came around and I rang Vanbitz who, after a detailed explanation of what I had worked out, got me to try a couple of things. Firstly to check that the switch on the inverter was still set to remote, it was. Secondly to check the fuse in the three pin plug that goes into the inverter out put. This was found to be a 5 amp fuse that had blown (kettle plus fan heater will be more that 5 amps). I rang Vanbitz back and they were a little baffled why only a 5 amp fuse was in there and 13 amps will be fine. So it appears that the inverter is in the ring main loop and if removed (or fuse blown) no circuit will be there any more.

Shropshire the forgotten county

As July draws to an end, it was finally time to begin heading towards southern Spain where we have planned to spend the coming winter. So we left Briarfields and headed north!.

Completely the wrong direction I know but we have a plan. Jacob my son has joined us for 3 weeks of his school holiday and I wanted to at least take him somewhere that might be interesting first.

We were sorry to leave all friends behind at Briarfields but looking forward to meeting up with a few of them later in the year or early next somewhere down in Spain or Portugal.

Whilst I had gone to collect Jacob, Ann had organised a buffet for all our friends at Briarfields. She had suddenly remembered that she had left some clothes in the drier and nipped off down to the laundry room to collect them. On her way back it dawned on her she had left the dogs alone with all the buffet food laid out on the table and kitchen sides. Opening the door expecting the worst she found them both laying on the floor having not touched a single thing. They were both suitably rewarded with sausage rolls.

I had chosen Telford to go to with Jacob for two good reasons. It has great potential of being interesting with the Iron Bridge and other museums in the area and secondly the site I have booked in at has been built to accommodate RV's with on pitch sewer connection and fresh water supply.

We did need to fill up on LPG on the way and this proved to be an issue as the motorway service station on the M5 at Strensham Services didn't have any again. To my surprise, we did make it to Telford services without having to fall back on the petrol. The only downfall with these services is that they were only designed for small vehicles such as cars and trucks. Trying to get a large RV in and out of the forecourt was not easy. Well getting in was OK but out meant I had to reverse out. From there it was only a short drive to Severn Gorge Park which is to be our base for the next 3 weeks.

I have no doubt I am like many other people in that I know Shropshire is a county but not only have I never, knowingly, been through it. In fact not even sure exactly where it is. Now this is a real shame because like me they are missing out on such a historically rich county with fantastic countryside.

Nestled between Wales to the West and Birmingham to the East and the Peak District to the North East it seems to have been forgotten and yet it's where things really started to happen in the 1700's for the Industrial Revolution in part thanks to the major change in making iron by Abraham Darby in 1709.

During our last week there, I heard from our friend Martin who had come to visit us for the weekend. He had been to see his physiotherapist who happened to be in Telford that same weekend he was visiting her boyfriend's family as she often does. Amazingly she had no idea that any of the museums and attractions were there at all. So seems that even the residents of Shropshire have forgotten their county. What chance do the rest of us have?

Severn Gorge Park is a lovely small site on the edge of a Parks Homes estate with 15 fully serviced pitches of varying sizes to accommodate motorhomes, caravans and even the big American RV's. It's strictly adults only and dog-friendly.

There is plenty to do in the area with museums, attractions, shopping, walking and all just a few miles away with excellent transport links. The bus service stops just outside the site. I thought the cost of bus travel was a little expensive but oddly the local taxi was very cheap. It worked out less than a pound more for two of us to travel to or from Telford city centre by taxi than on the bus. Waiting time for a taxi was blinking fast as well. They only gave me enough time to roll a fag and light it before they would be there. Stupid thing is I kept doing it, duh!

If you cross the road and cut through the small industrial estate you will find yourself on Silkin Way which looks like it was one of Beeching's casualties when he reshaped our railways in the sixties. It is now part of the National Cycle Network (route 55) and gives you very easy access to Telford centre just over two miles away in one direction and Madeley just over a mile away in the other direction with the first of the Blists Hill Museums just a bit further on. This provides some lovely cycling and walking with no steep grades due to it being an old railway line.

Do keep your eye open as you walk around the area as they seem to like to hide little gems. For example, I found a sculpture made from scrap metal hidden away of a horse and cart hidden behind some bushes and nearly fell over a sign on the Silkin Way made from an old train wheel.

In one of the brochures, I got from the reception for Blists Hill Victorian Town it states that you should allow 3+ hours for a visit here. You need a whole lot more. We could have spent the entire day there as it's absolutely fantastic and the best of the "Living Museums" I have been to. The costumed characters are great fun and really get into the spirit of the time period as well as explaining what life was like in Victorian times.

The town covers 52 acres and has been recreated to a very high standard. The first building you come across is the bank. Do make sure you go inside as it's here you can change some of your modern money for Victorian money specially minted for the town and can be used to purchase goods and freshly made food in the many shops in the town. The bank tellers will take time to explain what each coin is and its value.

They have done such a great job you really do feel you have been transported back to Victorian times. The only bit that spoiled this for me was in visiting the Forest Glen Refreshment Pavillon. Signs directed you around the to the entrance and through the doors where we were violently thrust back to a 21st century cafeteria. It's hard to believe now as I write this that it was such a shock but it really was and I lost all my appetite in that instant and we just left to search for something better.

Fortunately this didn't take to long as heading back up the hill to the main part of the town I spotted a sign to The New Inn Dining Rooms between the butchers and The New Inn public house. This was far more in keeping with the time period and we enjoyed a lovely meal and glass of ale.

Not only are there shops and various business premisses to explore but you will find the doors open to peoples homes where the residents will invite you in and chat to you about their lives. In one of the houses, I was reminded of my great grandmothers house and spent ages chatting to the lovely lady there about how everything was used and nothing was thrown away. They were far better at recycling than we are now. It was quite fascinating to see how the different classes lived then and you are reminded that there was a very distinct difference in society between them by the sign in the outfitters shop window that said:

Cast off Clothing
Lower classes may call after 5 o'clock.

It was such a shame we hadn't allowed enough time to visit and had to leave before we had seen everything and before we really wanted to and we will definitely have to return again.

The Iron Bridge which has been spanning the River Severn for over 230 years since 1779 is an impressive sight and is the oldest bridge over the Severn. It was just 14 years after its opening that a deluge of water and ice, from the sudden thaw of one of the most severe winters, that swept down the river taking out all of the bridges in its destructive path. All but the Iron Bridge which withstood this destructive force of nature and provided a direction marker for the future in Iron.

Today the bridge is still as impressive as the day it was unveiled and is one of the great symbols of the Industrial Revolution and dominates the beautiful small town bearing its name.

From the bridge, it is a 10 minute walk to the Museum of The Gorge where you can learn more about the industries of the area and the crucial linking role that transport played in supplying raw materials.

Back at the Victorian town they have a working replica of the first steam locomotive invented by Richard Trevithick in 1804 so it seemed only right that we should visit and ride on the Severn Valley Railway and enjoy what was to eventually develop from his brilliant invention.

The line is 16 miles long and snakes through some of the most stunningly beautiful scenery of the Severn Valley with 6 stations and 2 halts. There is plenty to do at each of the stops which provide a full day out for all the family. On the day we visited they had quite a number of locomotives in steam, the most I have ever seen on one line.

We joined the first train out of Bridgnorth and did the complete run to Kidderminster whilst planning which stations to stop at on our return. The best one to stop is Highley where they have The Engine House which has an impressive range of what they call "reserve collection" consisting of locomotives and specialist carriages including a Royal Mail sorting carriage.

It's here we also enjoyed a meal at the restaurant they have there where you can sit on the balcony overlooking the line and watch the trains going up and down the line back dropped by beautiful views across the Severn Valley.

Water Management

When you live in a house, as I did for 50 years, you never once give water a thought. After all, you go to the tap and it just pours out, as much as you like, and any excess or used water just disappears down the little hole in the sink or shower tray. Then there's the toilet, it's just there, ready whenever you are. It just needs a bit of a clean occasionally.

Once you have moved out of a house and into a Motorhome you then get to think about it a bit more. If you have a motorhome with the cassette toilets you need to add chemicals and empty it every few days, but not just anywhere, it has to be somewhere safe such as a chemical disposal point (CDP) which can be found on all campsites and aires and in Europe at many motorway service stations.

The same again with fresh and waste water. Your tanks can only hold so much water before you have to refill or empty. With our previous motorhome the fresh water tank only held 45 litres and I soon found out that having a shower used just about half of that.

The waste water is a little better in that it's easier to get rid of. Some camp sites even encourage you to dump your grey waste on or around your pitch especially if they have a drought issue.

With a RV, you have much bigger tanks to hold your fresh water and the waste tanks are big as well. Ours hold 250 litres of water with similar size grey and black tanks. This is great and means we can go a lot longer without having to empty and refill. Because the black tank is not a cassette toilet but a big sewer tank this makes it a bit more challenging, especially in the UK, to empty it. You need a ground level sewer access point to be able to empty it. As taking it around to the CDP at the back of the toilet block at a campsite is just not possible.

Fortunately, more and more sites are catering for RV's and this is gradually becoming less of an issue. On the Continent, this is no problem at all as every Aire and campsite we have found all have their CDP at ground level where you can easily access it.

There are alternatives to the emptying the toilet issue. You can purchase a tank that's on wheels where you can empty your black tank into it and then wheel it to the CDP round the back of the loos to empty that. However, how the hell you lift up something that heavy, don't forget it's not just water in there, so it can drain out is beyond me. The alternative to this is a device called a macerator which you connect to your 12 volt supply and the sewer outlet and it then breaks up any solids into tiny pieces and pumps it through a normal hose that will enable to use a CDP as far away as your hose will reach and go uphill as well. Personally this seems like an awful lot of effort especially if you find yourself on a site with an unsuitable CDP simply ask the wardens where their sewer manhole cover is, they must have one, and lift the cover as we did at Norden Farm.

Despite the size of our tanks, I was surprised how often we still needed to fill up and empty. We seemed to only last a week before the water tank was getting low and the grey tank was full. Filling the water tank was no real issues as you can easily locate a tap and on most sites with a long or even two hoses joined together you can refill without having to move. Emptying the waste tanks was another issue and does require moving to the service point.

What began to bother me was how was it going to be possible to wild camp for more than a week if we need to empty so often? I set about an experiment to see how this could be solved and really it was quite simple.

First off don't shower every day but every other day or even three days. In between have a strip wash. When you do shower use the navy shower technique, wet yourself down with the shower using just enough to get you wet, it only takes seconds, turn the shower off and soap yourself down. Then use the shower to rinse off but again use enough to rinse off not stand there for ages.

When washing your hands wet your hands turn the tap off, apply soap and then turn it on again to rinse off.

Do your dishwashing in a bowl and when finished pour the waste water down the toilet. There will be plenty of spare capacity in the black tank as there is no way you will fill it as fast as the grey.

We never drink the water out of the holding tank and always buy bottled water so this also keeps the usage down a little bit as well.

Now all this sounds like a lot of hassle and a pain after having an unlimited supply for all those years. But it's not really and becomes second nature very quickly. As a result, we can stretch out to around 3 weeks between services maybe longer if we try even harder.

Southwards

At last, it's time to start heading south with our final destination of Southern Spain taking in France and Germany on the way. We decided to take a little detour out to Germany mostly for the purpose of visiting some of Ann's relatives there.

First though I am going to take the opportunity of stopping a week in Kent so I can catch up on a few curries with my business partner Peter. I believe it's now 2 each we owe each other so that should be 4 in the week. I hope for Ann's sake we don't actually manage that many. According to Ann, I stink enough after just one, I think she might move out if I have 4.

On our way down to Kent, we had to make a very small detour to drop my son Jacob off in Crawley where he lives with his mum. We also made an attempt to fill up on LPG at Cobham services on the M25. Whilst they had it we couldn't fill up there as they had put the pump in a bad position. I could get to the pump but there was no way I would be able to make the turn in front of the shop to get out without reversing out the way we came in. There was no chance of this as the whole place was absolutely heaving. Cobham has always been busy ever since it has opened but was even worse today probably due to, like us, people having been stuck in very slow moving traffic for far too long.

This journey also enabled me to try out my new crash cam. The last one I bought was just a cheapie and had started to become unreliable and keep switching itself off on an annoyingly regular basis. So this time I decided to spend a bit more on one that should be better.

The DrivePro 220 by Transcend was indeed a lot more expensive but came with some cool additional features including built in WiFi with a free app so you can access the files and settings from a smart phone, lane departure warning system, forward coalition warning system, GPS built into the unit, parking mode and a good wide angle lens recording in full HD.

Despite the hold ups on the M25 we made quite good time and arrived at Bearstead Caravan Club Site mid afternoon. It's a neat and tidy site on sloping ground with all the usual facilities expected at a Caravan Club site and, of course, its strict rules regarding positioning on the pitch. It does kind of amuse me that you must park a particular way round with one corner exactly in line with the pitch marker which I know seems to annoy many others and really don't understand why. I personally do get it, it's mostly about maintaining the 6 meter rule they have in the UK but nowhere else in Europe.

The site is very expensive to stay on and probably the most expensive we have used in a long time. Having said that it is quite a big site with 69 pitches and the ability to cater for very large RV's like ours right down to those tiny tents that don't look big enough for someone to get into. There is a motorhome service point with a ground level dump point complete with taps for fresh and flush water.

It's also very conveniently located close to the M20 motorway which heads to and from the ports of Dover and Folkstone as well as the Channel Tunnel. Alas, because of this convenience there is a constant noise from the motorway close by which I would imagine continues all day and night. I can only imagine as noise like this really doesn't stop me sleeping and our RV is quite well insulated so cuts out a lot of the noise.

The channel crossing

We arose unpleasantly early to allow time to walk the girls, dump our waste and have more than enough time to get down to Dover for our 10:15am ferry over to Calais. It concerned me that because of the troubles with the migrants in Calais and the disgruntled aFerry staff who had all just lost their jobs, operation stack can be imposed without a great deal of notice and give us trouble in getting to the port on time.

There was no need to worry and we made it to the port in plenty of time. If fact so much earlier they put us on a much earlier crossing, bonus.

I was worried about leaving the girls alone in the RV for the crossing as they had never done it before and didn't know how they would cope with the movement of the ship at sea. Fortunately, it was a very smooth crossing and only once was there a noticeable, by me anyway, movement just as we entered the open sea from the harbour.

Having had a suitably expensive full English breakfast, finding out they no longer sold cigarettes on board, had a smoke out on the deck and a final coffee it was time to return to our vehicles on the parking deck. The girls had been absolutely fine and didn't seem to have been bothered by the experience at all.

We had been loaded right at the front on the left right next to a large tanker on our right and to be able to disembark would mean the taker would have to go out ahead of us as the bulkhead and door mechanisms on the left was partially blocking the lane we were in and because of our width we would need to pull over a little to the right. So the crew decided we were to go first ahead of the tanker. Why on earth would I expect otherwise.

As I slowly pulled out whilst turning slightly right as directed by the chap directing us he suddenly stopped us as he noticed we were going to catch the awning on some part of the tanker. He got me to turn slightly left to avoid the coalition and I almost made it out unscathed. My left-hand wing mirror hit a metal beam that is part of the ship and cracked the casing. Funny how this is the same side and thing that was damaged last year in our old Motorhome. Now I think about it, it also troubles me that we had trouble with 2 rear tyres on both vehicles as well. Spooky.

Germany

Having stoped over for one night in Belgium we headed for the town of Lemgo in Germany where we were planning to stop for two weeks. This is mainly because Ann's Aunt and Uncle live in the area and would give us a chance to catch up with them.

The biggest problem I have with Germany is that there is no Google Street View and means I cannot see in advance exactly where and what the site entrance looks like. As a result, we managed to miss the entrance and had to use a car park just down the road to turn around. This is one of the small issues with driving an 11 meter rigid body vehicle, you just can't turn around in the road.

We pulled into Camping Park Lemgo and were met by a very stern lady who complained that they had taken a booking for large vehicle and then wanted us to park in a spot where I could not make the turn to get into it without taking out a fence, then to another spot where we could not reach the electricity and then finally because I had turned around and could then make the turn easily back where she originally wanted us. Which as it turned out was an inconvenience to her as she could no longer see reception from the shed / shack (I am really at a loss as to what to call it) she lived in.

When we booked we were told the site had free WiFi but on asking the lady she said yes we have WiFi but it doesn't work. The following day we got speaking to the grounds keeper who turns out to be English and he said that it keeps needing to be reset and was not sure about it. He did let me take a look and I went round with him resetting the various routers etc and we got the internet up and running for a couple of days by which time it needed doing again. I mentioned this to him and he said he will do it later but never did for the rest of our stay.

The lady who runs the site has something of a reputation of being a bit of a dragon and watching her deal with other guests started to amuse me. If they didn't speak any German or felt they were idiots in any way (most people were) then she was very harsh and unfriendly with them.

It certainly appeared to me that she was far more interested in and friendly to the chickens she kept along with a cockerel. I had a great many plans on how this cockerel was best served for my dinner. Whilst I generally have no particular malice towards birds, this one was the exception. It wasn't just the fact I was woken at just after 5 every morning by its exceptionally loud crowing but the fact it also woke Sasha who then insisted I got up to take her for her morning walk so any sleep past this point was just not going to happen.

As always I don't do any research before visiting a place preferring to just explore in the early morning whilst walking the girls heading out in a different direction each morning.

I was very pleasantly surprised to find that Lemgo is a medieval town with buildings dating back to the late Gothic and Renaissance period which have been restored with a great attention to detail and as such looks absolutely beautiful and just 10 minutes walk away.

Because of the early morning wake up calls and the lack of WiFi we decided to cut our stay short and move on to France after only a week there instead on the planned two weeks. So we made plans to leave early on Saturday morning to get out of the town and back onto the Autobahn before the traffic got too busy.

It's at this point I realised I had made an error in my planning. I had used the timings from Google maps directions to calculate an approximate 5 to 6 hour drive between each site which would have been fine if I were able to go as fast as the speed limits would allow. The truth of the matter was I was only going to be doing half of that. This meant our next planned stop deep in the heart of France was a good 10 to 12 hours away. So some re-planning was needed.

France

Our next leg of our journey should have taken 5 hours but alas due to the bridge on the A1 that crosses the Rhine being closed to vehicles over 3.5 tonne and cut to just one lane not only was the traffic excessively heavy but we needed to take a very long detour which added an extra couple of hours.

By the time we reached Campéole Le Brabois it was quite late in the afternoon and the temperature was in excess of 30 degrees so we were all glad to get pitched up and out sitting in the shade of a tree with a cold drink.

It's a large site of a 170 pitches with a good mixture of shaded and sunny pitches. We were lucky to be given a pitch which was partly shaded so had the best of both worlds and suited us just fine.

It seems to be used mostly as a transit site with the majority of people staying just one night on their way south to the sun or north back home. This is a shame as there is such a lot to offer in the area and we were glad we stayed put for a couple of weeks.

It's situated in a great location at the top of the hill above Nancy with the Parc de Brabois to the rear of the site which offers some beautiful easy walking and some stunning views over Nancy.

Nancy itself is a fascinating and diverse city which has everything to offer in great abundance including art, history, gastronomy and shopping.

The old part of the city which apparently dates back to medieval times is well worth a visit and it was my fortune that on Sunday I chose to visit was the day in August they hold the Flea Market in the old city and the streets were crowded with stalls selling everything you could possibly think of and then some things you would never think of.

One of the days I spent in Nancy was a Sunday and whilst the old part of the city was bustling with activity the rest of it was deserted with all the shops closed. It's here that it suddenly dawned on me that we should be moving to each new destination on a Sunday and not Saturday. As unlike the UK Europe still pretty much shuts down and rests on the seventh day. It will be so much easier to navigate roads within towns on a Sunday with hardly any traffic around.

It no longer amazes me how people can have so much trouble with Sat-nav's. I quite often read on the various forums and Facebook about people's woes and complaints how their Sat-nav has let them down. Even myself with a very technical background in computers and programming have managed to cock it up twice now. The first time I picked up the wrong piece of paper with the address of a show ground in Norfolk to get almost there and realise were heading to the wrong one. The one we were booked to go to a month later. It so happens they were both in Norfolk so didn't spot my mistake when entering the postcode.

The second mistake took much longer to spot. Having traveled through France, Belgium, The Netherlands, Germany and back into France not once going on a toll road but still all motorways. This was quite disappointing me as I had purchased a Toll Box from tolltickets.com and was waiting for my first chance to try it out. It's on this latest leg from Nancy to Mâcon that I really began to wonder as we started going through towns and villages on some fairly narrow roads.

After several hours of this we stopped for a break in a large lorry park on the outskirts of a town where it occurred to me to check the Sat-nav settings. Some weeks back when travelling down from Telford to Kent I had set it to avoid toll routes to be sure it wouldn't take me across the Dartford Crossing and forgot change it back after.

With the Sat-nav properly configured the rest of our journey time to Mâcon was halved as we were re-routed via toll roads. We approached the first of the toll booths entering the toll road and drove all the way up to the barrier and sat there as nothing happened for several seconds and just as I was beginning to think 'bugger it don't work' and I am not close enough to the intercom to use it without getting out there was a loud beep from the toll box and the barrier opened. Phew, what a relief. It turns out if it's not used for a long while, or in this case never been used, it can take several seconds to get it's self-organised.

We stayed at Camping Municipal De Macon and just like our last site was used mostly as a transit site although this time with good reason. Firstly its located close to the A6 and A40 motorways. Secondly there are two big supermarkets close by (Lidl and Auchan) giving you an opportunity to stock up.

Also unlike Nancy, Mâcon has little to offer. To be honest its tired and uninteresting, which is a shame as it sits on the river Saône and could have so much potential. I managed to find one museum which I initially mistook as potentially a maritime museum until I realised before I got there it was actually a museum of a famous French politician and poet Alphonse de Lamartine. I didn't bother to go, it looked closed anyway,

Its saving grace is there is plenty of shopping, there is a regular bus service to and from the town centre and there are some beautiful walks close to the site along the banks of the river.

it was time to move on partly because there was little to interest us there but mostly because the weather was rubbish and quite chilly. We would normally dump our waste and fill up with fresh water before leaving a site but because access to the service point was difficult we thought we would not bother but stop on one of the Aires where they have a service point.

This was a bit of a mistake as we quickly discovered that travelling with a tank partly full of poo, sloshing around, smells really bad. Fortunately an Aire not too many miles away enabled us to sort that out. Well, that was the plan.

Alas, they had closed their service point and had to carry on smelling bad. The next one, an hour or so away, we couldn't get access to due to a height barrier, so still further, we get to enjoy our pungent journey. We did finally find one and was able to get rid of our waste. Never again will we leave a site without dumping first.

Due to the awful weather in northern and central France I decided that we would head all the way down to the south in one hit and hopefully better weather. When we left Mâcon it was dull and overcast. Slowly as we headed south the clouds began to break apart and the sun started shining through until a good few hours later we were driving under the most beautiful cloudless blue sky and the temperature had risen to the mid to high twenties. Not that stifling, humid, heat you get in the north but that lovely dry Mediterranean heat.

Whilst it was warm and sunny we did notice that it was quite windy by the way the trees were being battered around. Just how windy we didn't realise until we stopped to fill up with LPG. The service station we stopped at was being very battered around with signs banging and the covers on the pumps rattling in the wind. The RV was also being rocked from side to side as I was filling up. I was most impressed at how well it coped driving in such high winds but then again at seven and a half tonnes and very wide its going to take a lot to bother it.

Back on the motorway having just left the service station the wind caught us from an angle that lifted the engine cowling inside the cab and I was blasted by extremely hot air. The cowling has never sat quite right and had been impossible to align the clips on both sides and as a result my right leg was quite often treated to a hot air treatment enough to ensure driving in shorts was not a great option. But this was a whole new escalation to the problem.

Driving along whilst trying to keep the cover down was a ridiculous challenge so we pulled over in the next Aire to see if we can do something. Ann had the idea of completely removing it then reattach it starting on my side first, getting it clipped in then try and clip her side in. After a lot of pushing, shoving, swearing, kneeling, swearing some more for good measure we finally did it and got it secured properly for the first time ever. I changed into my shorts to celebrate.

At the end of our seven and a bit hour drive, we arrived at Camping Le Fun. It's rubbish. It's in the middle of nowhere and with the exception of July and August they don't have any restaurant or snack bar open. There is nothing to do unless you're into wind surfing and have your own gear. The swimming pool is not heated (even though they say it is on the website).

I liked it. The pitches are really big and bordered by shrubbery, because it wasn't in the high season the site was almost empty and very quiet except to the railway line close by but the noise from that was just the right side of too loud so was not really an issue. Lighting at night is very limited almost to the point of why bother which is great for sitting or laying out at night to gaze at the stars.

I would have carried on liking it if it were not for the fact we ended up trapped inside for most of the week. It was sunny and warm with a beautiful clear blue sky, but the wind just didn't let up for just about the whole week. It was relentless, and with gusts up to 50 MPH just made it impossible to sit outside. Not only that we had to keep the slide-out in to protect the topper from being damaged.

So after a week of confinement it was time to move on and into Spain.

Spain

Unlike last year, we didn't take the drive over the old road through the mountain passes but entered Spain via the E15. To be honest, I would have enjoyed the challenge of getting this new beast round the mountain passes but there was no way I would be able to stand the screaming that would loudly emanate from my darling wife.

We headed for a site just the other side of Barcelona which according to their website and the reviews I had read had a lot of promise as being a good site.

It's not quite so easy to get LPG in Spain as it is in France with Repsol petrol stations being the only company in Spain with the contract to sell Autogas and not all their stations have it. This means a little research and planning is required as the majority of the ones selling it are not the ones on the Autovías and Autopistas. Fortunately, there is a great resource on the internet called myLPG.eu which is a community driven website listing the vast majority of LPG stations throughout Europe. The best thing on there is the route planner that will show you all the LPG stations close to your route.

So all should be hunky dory with just one little diversion off the big main highways to get some LPG. Well, it wasn't. Back somewhere in France I had worked out it was best to drive on a Sunday when the roads are a bit quieter and towns and cities are pretty much empty and PETROL STATIONS CLOSED. Whoops hadn't thought of that.

Much to my amazement we made it to Villanova Park with still some LPG to spare, although not much as we were well into the reserve.

Villanova Park is a big resort type site with a large number of cabins available as well, which seem to be owned by several different holiday companies. There is also a large area that is dedicated to seasonal/permanent pitches and looks like is owned exclusively by Spanish families.

The facilities are great with 2 outdoor pools, 1 indoor pool / spa, a couple of bars, a very good restaurant, a takeaway place plus a range of sports and fitness facilities.

Just outside the entrance are 2 bus stops one with a regular service to the local city Vilanova i la Geltrú and the other which will take you to Barcelona again, a regular service. A small word of warning, don't ask in reception about the bus service. Ann asked about the service to Barcelona on a weekend and was told they don't run on the weekend. I was sure I had been told by one of the bus drivers I was chatting to one morning when walking the dogs that they did. That Saturday I caught the bus to Barcelona.

Barcelona is no different to any other big city throughout Europe with the obvious exception that there is more outside seating in restaurants and cafés that in northern cities. They have a couple of open top bus tours that you can get on and off as you please but alas on the day I visited there was a constant threat of rain so I didn't bother. As it turned out, it never did rain, oh well. Anyway, my main purpose for the visit was to do some shopping for a few things I needed including a new iPhone so as far as I am concerned it was a successful trip.

Vilanova i la Geltrú on the other hand is still classed as a city but not a sprawling metropolis like Barcelona. It's very culturally rich with a few museums, art galleries and libraries all within walking distance of the train station.

The closest, right next to the station, and to my mind the best is "Museu del Ferrocarril de Catalunya" which is a museum of the history of the Spanish railway. They have an impressive number of locomotives from early steam to more recent electric and diesel. It struck me as interesting that the main influence of trains was from America and not Britain as I would have expected.

It was during our stay here at Vilanova Park that I was woken in the early hours by the storm from hell. The rain, well rain is a serious understatement, it would be better described as a waterfall from the sky. It was so dense you could not see further than a dozen or so yards. The road outside wasn't, it had turned into a fast flowing river that even the very deep drains along and across the road could not swallow quickly enough. And that's not even the best bit. The lightening was fast and continuous. Nothing like the storms I have experienced in my 50 odd years so far where a big storm will create a flash of lightning every 1 or 2 minutes, this was literally every 1 or 2 seconds with thunder louder than mortar shells going off close by.

The following morning we discover that the storm really was right on top of us when opening the door we find a tree had been struck a brought down just a few yards away from us. Fortunately, it had fallen away from us otherwise we will have suffered some damage.

Early on a Sunday morning on a Spanish bank holiday weekend it was time to go to empty our tanks and fill the fresh water up ready to move on to our next destination.

As we are attempting to leave the site through the, we only just fit through, gate some numpty has parked some 15 meters away. Plenty of room for a car and caravan to go past or a standard motorhome but for our 11 meter rigid body it's going to be tight. Alas, too tight and I manage to catch the running light on the rear on the gate post and smash the cover off.

We are still a full two weeks ahead of our originally planned schedule which is good as will allow us to make an additional stop to visit some old friends later on.

After a days uneventful travelling, we arrived at Marjal Costa Blanca Camping & Resort. As it was so close to the AP7 motorway my satnav thought my destination was actually on the motorway itself and told me I had reached my destination whilst traveling at 80kph along the motorway. Just as panic tried to set in I looked up to see a massive sign which said Marjal Camping Resort with an arrow indicating to leave at the next junction and from there it was well signposted.

Marjal is a big site, and I mean really big. Every pitch is a full-service pitch which means you have on pitch water, sewerage, as well as electric hook up and a TV point that carries the main channels for Spain, France, Germany and England. If you don't have a cable to connect your TV then the supermarket has long ones for just €4. Needless to say, the wife was very happy being able to watch her soaps and the X Factor.

We found there were a couple of downsides to the site. The supermarket is not very big and so is great for most essentials but not everything you would need for a long stay. There is no public transport close by and the nearest town, Catral, is 2.5 kilometres away.

Despite the fact it is probably the most expensive place we have stayed at in quite a long while we stayed put for 5 weeks.

Insurance

This is something we all know we must have however there are many "Full Timers" who are seriously misguided and in an attempt to keep the cost low they are creative with what they tell their insurance company.

Creative, as far as insurance companies are concerned, is just another word for lying or at least failing to declare ALL the facts in their fullest. The end result of this is their insurance is invalid and they don't have any insurance at all.

A couple I met a few months back told me they keep their premium down by telling their insurance company that they live at their son's address when in fact they have never lived there they just use his address for the post.

If the worst were to happen and their motorhome was written off, there is a good chance that the loss adjusters will look into their claim and find that they do not live there as they stated. The result of this will be they will not get a penny out of the company and they will not only have lost their transport but their home and maybe all their belongings as well.

I fully understand their desire to reduce the premiums as not only is it difficult to get a full-timers insurance policy, so far I have only been able to find one (http://www.motorhomefacts.com/motorhome-insurance.html), and it's very expensive at double the cost of a standard policy.

For our RV, that weighs in at a hefty £1,400 for the year. This does include fully comprehensive insurance plus breakdown cover anywhere in Europe.

Why it is double the cost does mystify me as I would have thought that full-timers were a lower risk than those who leave parked on their drive for most of the year. After all it's never left empty, we have all our precious belongings with us and it's our home. As a result, we are far more careful when driving than if it was just a holiday vehicle where you have a home to return to if anything happens. I have also found I do considerably fewer miles than I did when we had a house. So surely we are a much lower risk? I have a sneaking suspicion that because it's a small market in comparison and so few offer it as a policy that they hike the price.

Old Friends

Our next stop gave us a chance to visit friends we made last year during Christmas at Cabopino, Tim and Pippa, and, as it happens, friends, we made back at Briarsfield in Cheltenham, Mark, Fiona and Chester the dog, happened to be staying there at the time. This was not a planned stop and had to be kept fairly short as they did not have any facility to dispose of our black waste.

Our journey from Marjal to Cabopino took us along the A-92N and some of the most stunning scenery we have every seen. We travelled over and through some impressive mountain ranges. The weather conditions added to the spectacle with cloud formations hanging onto the tops of mountains making it look like an enormous wave of crystal white snow crashing over the top and frozen in time.

We had telephoned Pippa the day before and had been told that Cabopino has another gate that they use to let larger vehicles in as the entrance through the automatic barriers is very tight. So on arrival, I stopped on the road and Ann went into book us in and get them to open the gates for us.

Whilst they have a few very large pitches, more than big enough for even the largest of RV's, even with a trailer attached, navigating through the site is very tight indeed. Fortunately, for us, the one difficult turn we would have had to make had its adjacent pitch unoccupied so we cut through that.

During our visit, Cabopino was making a lot of changes to the site. Firstly all the site roads were relaid with tarmac and the larger pitches down the bottom of the site was being relaid and levelled. Apparently they will also be making the entrance bigger and more accessible which includes moving the restaurant at the entrance to the other end of the site. I am guessing all this is to make it more accessible for RV's. Let's hope they also sort out the black waste dumping problem as well.

It seems that not only the site is having major improvements but also the sand dunes and car park over the road. They had already put some extensive boardwalks all along the top of the dunes with several access points down to the beach and into the car park, which they were busy relaying.

Our two-week stopover flew by and after making arrangements for us all to meet over Christmas at our next site near Cadiz it was time to move on.

Our journey was to take us past Gibraltar and we really couldn't pass up the opportunity to make an overnight stopover near the rock and nip over the border to pick up some cheap booze and cigarettes.

Last year, when visiting the rock, I had driven past the nearby football stadium where I had heard they allow motorhomes to park overnight for a small fee and it is there we headed for.

From there it is a short 15 minute walk to the border with the beach just over the road. An overnight stay is €3 and doesn't have any facilities at all.

Ann made a couple of trips over the boarder once walking and using a local taxi to return and once on the electric bicycle, which ran out of power 5 minutes down the road on her way there, returning with various goodies including a supply of tobacco for me and some English treats.

We sat and watched as the sun went down over the Mediterranean and was treated to some of the most beautiful oranges and blues as the light gradually shifted towards darkness. This is well worth another visit just for that. I think if it were not for our booking at Camping Roche we probably would have stayed a few more nights.

The day of our visit the local football team had a match that evening and we were somewhat concerned and not sure what to expect. We needed have worried as the fans all turned up and filled the carpark around us quite quietly and after the match all just left equally as quietly. No idea if they won or not and if that had any bearing on their quiet departure.

Rural Spain

Our next stop is to be our base for Christmas. This was supposed to be close enough to Gibraltar so that with the use of a hire car I can easily ferry backwards and forwards picking up and dropping off at the airport the three people flying in to see us all at different times.

However, this plan was devised at the same time as when I was planning the whole adventure and as you know already know I made a complete hash of it over distances and timings. Yes, you guessed it, this was no different.

Camping Roche turns out to a 1 hour 30 from Gibraltar which was considerably further than I thought it would be. It's also in the middle of an agricultural area with farms and small holdings all around us.

How lovely and peaceful, you would imagine. Lovely yes, peaceful NO. In Spain with every farm and smallholding comes guard dogs. Not guard dogs like the ones you see on the TV that only appear when you try to trespass onto a property. No these are just ordinary dogs that bark at anything that moves or might move in a half mile radius around the property.

The early morning is started off in the traditional rural way with all the cockerels in the area have a good shout announcing the rising of the sun and the day proceeds with the calls of donkeys interspersed with the odd whinny of a horse. The only ones that are quiet are the cows, guess they think there is enough without their input.

At least, the nights will be quite, and they would have been, had it not been for a cockerel close by that has mental health issues. He just doesn't stop from sunset to sunrise. I eventually worked out that it was the moon that seemed to confuse the retarded bird as when we had a moonless night he seemed quieter.

We had booked a double pitch so we had plenty of room for our beast and I figured if the pitches were not long enough we could pitch up at an angle across the two. This would have been great had they not got trees and plants between each pitch. It was just long enough, with the bike removed off the back, but impossible to get into without a lot of shuffling and using the pitch opposite and the one next to that.

They have a nice big area for waste disposal including a ground level black waste drain but getting to it was a real challenge as they have it near the back of the site and access to it was narrow with 90 degree bends that anything over 8 meters was going to have great difficulty with without making use of the pitches on the corners.

Never the less we did our first run up there and fortunately, at the time, the site was mostly empty so those vital corner pitches were unoccupied. The problem was coming back we had to squeeze back into our pitch which is when I managed to scrape the side of the RV at the rear on a tree.

A few days before we had been chatting to our neighbour who also had a RV and had a macerator to dump his waste down the drain on the pitch. With him making it all look so simple and convenient and with the game of shove with the tree I finally admitted that we really should get one. He did say it would quickly become my best friend and most useful device I would own.

It arrived in the post quite quickly and having been up the road to a machine and hardware shop, turned out handy to be in an agricultural area, to buy 20 meters of 1-inch hose and jubilee clips, I got everything set up. My kind neighbour came over to take me through what he found was the best way of doing a dump.

This was all a lot easier and quicker than I thought it would be. Since getting the macerator and writing this, I have used it whenever possible, and have to say it's much easier than having to move the RV.

Having hired a car, it was time to make my first run to Gibraltar airport, to pick up my youngest son Jacob. Having left in plenty of time to meet him and drove the 90 minutes to Gibraltar, I was just about to go through border control when I realised I had left my passport behind. Panic set in as I realised there was no way I could make it all the back to get it. As I approached the Spanish border control I stopped and spoke to the police and explained the situation and they said no problem for them but then said "they may have" pointing to the UK police. As I approached the UK border control, I stopped and started to explain where I was abruptly told to return to Spain immediately.

I had no choice but to go back and get my passport. I made a desperate call to Ann who said she will ring the airport and try to get a message to him when he arrives.

I was so glad I had hired a bigger car this time round that could do the maximum speed allowed on the autovista and with some very aggressive accelerating at each junction I managed to shave nearly 30 minutes off the journey each way. It was also a blessing that Spanish roads are nearly always empty so had no hold ups because of traffic.

If it wasn't for the fact all my concentration was absorbed by driving as fast as allowed I would have gone out of my mind with worry. This was Jacobs first trip away alone and the thought of hm finding himself in a strange place with no one meeting him would have probably broken me.

Having finally got to the airport 2 hours late and not messing about with the pay and display, I thought stuff it I don't care, I ran through one of the 2 entrances and bumped straight into my son in the doorway. He was totally bemused by my panicked face and profuse apologies. Turns out he had only just arrived as was delayed by 90 minutes at Gatwick. Oh and he never got the message.

Christmas

As last year, our very dear friend Martin flew over to join us for Christmas and a few days after boxing day Pippa and Tim, who we met at Cabopino last year, drove over from there to rent a cabin and spend a few days with us all.

After last year's bizarre experience of a Christmas in the sun, I would have thought it would not be quite so bizarre an experience. So to make sure it was equally bizarre Ann cooked a traditional Christmas dinner with all the trimmings and we all sat down to enjoy the delicious spread outside in the sun.

I swear it tasted so much better being eaten al fresco although again it just didn't feel like a Christmas day. Seriously though I am not complaining.

Just after new year my son, Nathaniel flew over to spend a week with us. Of course, none of these flights to and from Gibraltar coincided even slightly and I ended up going backwards and forwards a total of six times. You could say seven but the first time I didn't get over the border so I am not counting that one.

This has been another year in which we have learned so much and I suspect our education is far from over.